FADING ROCKSTAR SYNDROME

SURVIVING EGOS, CHAOS & BAD DECISIONS

P. K. KOVICH

Fading Rockstar Syndrome
Surviving Egos, Chaos & Bad Decisions
By P. K. Kovich

Cover design by P. K. Kovich
Formatted and published by Still Not Famous Books
https://stillnotfamousbooks.com

This is a work of fiction and satire. All characters, names, bands, and venues are either imaginary or used in a fictional context. Any resemblance to actual persons, places, or incidents - past, present, or still holding on - is coincidental and not intended.
Reader discretion and a sense of humor are advised.

For inquiries: contact@stillnotfamousbooks.com
ISBN (Paperback): 978-1-7640648-0-4
First Edition

Contents

To my loving wife - *who has endured years of me endlessly tweaking synth patches, obsessing over plugins, and insisting that playing with beat machines and MIDI controllers is "real work" (despite having nothing to show for it).*

And to almost all my musician friends...

Without your questionable decisions, stubborn habits, and complete refusal to read manuals, this book wouldn't exist.

A Note to scholars, critics, and those of you who correct people mid-sentence...

Buckle up. This ain't your professor's memoir. This book is about musicians and contains traces of grammar crimes. Please read at your own risk. I'm just here to tell a story.

Welcome to the Madness

Let's face it. At some point, you've either been in a band, tried to start one, or spent enough time around musicians to realize that bands are barely functional social experiments, held together by duct tape, passive-aggressive tension, and the vague promise of making it big.

If you've ever endured a rehearsal where the guitarist refused to turn down, the drummer launched into an unsolicited 10-minute solo, or the singer demanded "just a little more reverb," congratulations - you already understand the *Fading Rockstar Syndrome* universe.

This is not a guide to success. You won't learn how to write a hit song, master your instrument, or survive the treacherous waters of the music industry. Instead, it will mercilessly expose some of the most absurd, ego-fueled disasters musicians bring upon themselves - all with a wink, a laugh, and just enough truth to sting.

I've spent a lifetime around musicians - some I've known since we were kids, long before they picked up an instrument. Others I met along the way, watching quirks evolve, obsessions spiral, and the refusal to admit fault become an art form. Some are still my closest friends - the ones I see and talk to nearly every day.

This book exaggerates it all - on purpose. But you'll recognize every bit of it if you've been in a band long enough. Some of you will laugh. Some of you might get offended. Either way, if you see yourself in these pages... Well, that's between you and your ego. I'll let you two sort that out.

And if you don't see yourself in any of it... maybe you were the one holding it all together.

For readability (and to spare you from seeing 'audio engineer' a hundred times), we're going with 'sound guy.' Not out of disrespect - just practicality. That's what most people call them anyway. And if the sound guy ever reads this book, he'll pretend not to like it - then recommend it to every other tech he knows. Likewise, the keyboardist will occasionally be the 'keys guy' because, let's face it, even their own band treats them like a mystical synth wizard operating in another dimension.

Just so we're clear - every role in this book is filtered through one biased, overcaffeinated perspective: mine.
I know - sometimes the bassist is the control freak. The guitarist is the genius. The singer keeps it tasteful. And the drummer can actually read notation. But that's not the point. This is satire. If the shoe fits, wear it. If it doesn't... maybe you just drove the van. I'm just throwing bones here - loose sketches of band chaos for you to flesh out with your own memories, grudges, and unfinished demos.

So whether you're a bassist who just realized you've been inaudible for five years, a singer still waiting for your big break, or a guitarist currently tweaking your perfect tone for the ninth time today - this book is for you. And if you're not a musician but bravely nodding through terms like "reverb," "DI," and "feedback," don't worry, there's a glossary at the end. It's surprisingly informative, deeply unhelpful, and accidentally educational.

Welcome to *Fading Rockstar Syndrome* - where no one is safe, and everyone gets what's coming. Now let's talk about how badly you're screwing this up...

Chapter 1

The Master of Blending into Oblivion

Playing bass in a band full of attention seekers

"For those who seek glory,

It is not seized in the blaze of solos nor the desperate theatrics of stage dives...

True power lies in the unshaken - the ones who resist the urge to climb atop the drum kit for attention. For yours, it is a craft not measured by the eyes it draws but by the chaos it prevents.

Not all heroes take center stage. Some remain unseen in the shadows, while others fight for the spotlight. Because when the fog clears and the lights go out, you are still there, holding the whole mess together. Invisibly. Like a legend."

- ***The Ghost in the Mix***

When the Spotlight Didn't Call, but the Low-end Did

Let's be honest - when you first picked up your instrument, you didn't exactly choose the bass. The bass chose you.

Think back. The guitarist was already lost in daydreams of face-melting solos before even figuring out how to tune while the drummer pounded on the furniture like a caffeinated caveman. The singer perfected hair flips like he was auditioning for a shampoo commercial. And you? Someone handed you a four-stringed plank and said,

"Look, we already have two guitarists. We need you to hold down the low-end."

And just because you're reliable, you took one for the team. Thus began your noble quest - steady, essential, and completely invisible.

You're the pulse - the quiet force holding it all together. And yet, despite your quiet heroism, your stage presence lands somewhere between 'a roadie' and 'that guy who wandered up to help with the drum kit.' This isn't a TED Talk on embracing your groove. No one's here to pat you on the back and say you're doing great, champ.

You already bring the groove. Now it's time to get some presence - without, you know... wearing a fedora. Because being overlooked sucks. Without you, the music doesn't just lose something - it falls apart. While they chase the spotlight, you make the music feel alive. It's just egos in a desperate search for structure.

The Bassist's Paradox: Invisible, Yet Indispensable

You're the heartbeat - felt more than heard, steady enough to keep everything together. The foundation that stops the band from collapsing into a chaotic mess of self-indulgent solos and questionable tempo shifts. But here's the catch: being solid doesn't make you noticeable.

In your head, you're the mysterious backbone of the band, the calm, collected groove master anchoring the chaos while the crowd whispers, "Who's that cool guy holding it all together?"

Reality check: To most of the audience, you're background noise. A blurry figure, lurking off to the side of the stage, noticed only when your amp buzzes, or you stop playing, and the entire song suddenly feels weird.

If the guitarist introduced the band and somehow skipped you - again - that's a sign. If your family showed up and later said:

"I think I saw you. Were you the one behind the big speaker?"

Another sign.

It's time to face it.

So let's break it down - why no one's noticing you, how your bandmates steal the spotlight, and most importantly, how to flip the script.

The Art of Being Essential and Ignored at the Same Time

Let's talk about how your band completely undermines you. You're not just a musician - you're part of a chaotic social experiment where everyone thinks they're the star. And somehow, as the bassist, you've become the parsley sprig on a plate of musical excess.

Essential? Completely.

Acknowledged? Absolutely not.

While you're holding everything together, the drummer hits the kit as if it owes him money. In your eyes, he's a human earthquake, a percussive force of nature with an absolute zero of self-control, filling every available space with rolls, crashes, and questionable timing decisions. You figure he sees you as his rhythmic partner. He doesn't. He's too busy overplaying even to realize you exist.

The lead guitarist isn't much better. He treats every gig like a one-person audition for a sponsorship deal that will probably never happen. He's drowning the mix in reverb, divebombing solos into the void, and making deep, emotional guitar faces at the crowd as if his pentatonic scale choices are changing lives. You assume he barely notices you. "Oh, right. Do we have a bassist? Cool. Do you, like... do solos, bro?"

Until the moment he gets lost mid-song and looks at you like a confused child in a grocery store.

The rhythm guitarist is next - the guy hammering out the same three power chords with the enthusiasm of someone who just learned "Wonderwall." While you're locking everything down, he's convinced his slightly out-of-tune G chord is the secret sauce behind the band's greatness. He plays like a human backing track with anxiety. But don't expect him to appreciate the work you're doing. The sound guy has been slowly turning him down all night, and he hasn't even noticed.

And the keys guy - the synth sorcerer - a self-proclaimed master of "atmosphere." He doesn't just play notes; he creates textures. Or so he says.

Half the time, you're convinced he's just pressing one key and letting the machines do the work. He exists in a different universe, lost in a haze of synth pads and reverb tails, making adjustments mid-song while the rest of the band is just trying to finish the damn track. You try to sync up with him, but he thinks you don't get music. You know for a fact he doesn't get rhythm.

And then, the singer. A mic-holding peacock who spends more time twirling scarves and making exaggerated hand gestures than actually keeping time. He's too busy winking at the audience, flipping his hair, and demanding more reverb to acknowledge that you are making his job possible. But the second your bass cuts out? Pure panic. Suddenly, he realizes that without you, his carefully crafted rockstar moment collapses into an awkward, rhythmless mess. For a moment, he sees you. Then the song ends, and you're invisible again.

While the roadie flirts with the merch girl, the guitarist basks in post-show praise. The drummer soaks through yet another shirt, and the singer gets treated like a deity. You're in the corner, wrapping cables - quietly questioning every life decision that led you here.

Groove Alone Won't Save Your Love Life

You didn't pick up the bass for attention. You told yourself it was about the music - the groove, the feel, the pure satisfaction of locking in with the drummer. But let's be honest. At some point, you thought,
'This has to be attractive to someone, right?'

It could be that old myth about the primal allure of rhythm. Maybe it was blind optimism. Either way, you figured playing bass came with an aura - a quiet magnetism. Yeah. About that. You've spent years standing in the corner, locked into the pocket, silently hoping your low-end mastery radiates some raw, undeniable appeal. It's not. And it never was. You might see yourself as the incredible, mysterious foundation of the band, but from across the room, you're just a guy standing suspiciously still.

At first, you leaned into the quiet thing. You told yourself it made you intriguing. The silent type. The one with depth. You imagined a scenario where someone would glance at you mid-set, see your steady focus, and think,
'*Wow, he must be deep.*'
They don't.
Silence doesn't scream mystery. It whispers, *'Wait... is the bassist even plugged in?'*
And the only person picking up on your vibe is the sound guy - who, at best, might give you a respectful nod before returning to the singer's ever-growing list of reverb demands.
Fine. Maybe it's not about mystery. Perhaps you'll let the music speak for itself. A solid, tasteful groove will do all the work for you. You picture her locking eyes with you mid-set, thinking,
'The emotional depth of that C minor walk. He must have layers.'

She's not. She's watching the guitarist climb his amp mid-solo like a jungle gym while the drummer looks like he's actively fighting his limbs for survival.

Over on your side of the stage, you're quietly thumping your E string like you're inspecting a loose floorboard. You're holding the song together, but nobody's holding onto you. Blending in too much has consequences. So maybe you can try standing out. But... not like that. Remember when you thought a fedora would make you look mysterious? You paired it with sunglasses. Indoors... The idea - add flair. Finally, get noticed. The result? Less rockstar and more jazz professor, aggressively cornering students after class.

Maybe you even took it a step further - experimented with a slap solo during a ballad, spun around dramatically only to nearly take out the keyboardist's rig...

Well, at least you tried.

If you picked up this book hoping for some bass-specific dating hacks, you might need something closer to *"Zen and the Art of Making Eye Contact While Playing Whole Notes."*

But if you're here to actually become unforgettable - the kind of bassist they remember long after the set - then keep going. There's a way. You just have to play it right.

Pickup Lines That Will Fail

(But You Keep Trying Anyway)

You've convinced yourself that being a bassist is an automatic charm generator. The groove, the smooth playing, the low-end mastery - the full seduction package, in theory. No need for flashy solos or full-on dramatic stage antics. Just deep frequencies and raw, primal sex appeal.

Except it doesn't work that way. Still, that won't stop you from trying. After all, you are the backbone of the music, the pulse that holds everything together. Surely, someone must appreciate that. Tonight, as you lean against the bar after soundcheck, sipping a lukewarm beer, you tell yourself - this is your moment.

She was nodding her head during the set. Maybe she even glanced in your direction once or twice. Maybe it wasn't at you specifically - perhaps she was just watching the drummer suffer a mild cardiac event behind his kit - but still... There's a chance. You straighten your posture, adjust your jacket - as if it matters - and casually slide in next to her. Low and mysterious. That's the approach. Just enough weight in your voice to make it intriguing.

"I play bass."

She blinks quickly. Twice. No reaction. You wait, expecting some acknowledgment, maybe a flicker of curiosity. Nothing. Just a polite, vaguely confused nod. Alright. Maybe she didn't hear you. You might need to reinforce the idea.

"You know... essential but misunderstood."

Another nod. The kind of response people give when they're unsure if they just got hit on or asked for directions.

You need something more substantial. Something that lets her experience the sheer power of the rhythm section.

"Do you feel my low end?"

Her polite smile tightens. Not only does she not feel it, but she is suddenly very interested in her drink. You panic. Course correction is needed. Humor. That's your best hope.

"You can't spell 'bass' without ass... if you think about it."

Stop. Right. There.

She blinks again, this time slower. You can see the gears turning behind her eyes. That was not the move. You scramble. Try to recover.

"I bring the vibe. So... you into frequencies or what?"

Ah yes... Seduction via waveform analysis. Very smooth. Confident and sexy, only if you were trying to flirt with an oscilloscope. She shifts in her seat. Not closer. Away.

Maybe she's more into the intellectual side of music. Theory. Structure. That has to count for something, right?

"I control the entire emotional depth of the song."

She takes another sip. A long one. The longest sip of her life. This is slipping away. You need a grand gesture. Something that communicates both musical prowess and raw charisma.

"I slap, I pop... but I'm also into subtle fingerstyle work."

Well, it looks like you'll be playing fingerstyle alone tonight. She now looks like someone who just received an unexpected call from their insurance provider.

This is getting ridiculous. One last move, you tell yourself. The Closer.

The phrase that will turn this around.

"I once tuned to drop C. Wanna find out why?"

She absolutely does not. At this point, you should quit trying so desperately. But you don't.

"The band only works because I'm holding down the groove. Speaking of holding down..."

Her drink goes down. Fast. Faster than you thought it was possible. Her eyes dart around the room. Not in excitement. In search of an exit.

And then, when you think you've hit rock bottom, you deliver the final, desperate attempt.

"Ever felt a G major arpeggio in your soul?"

For a moment, she looks at you. A pause. A flicker of acknowledgment. Then she turns and asks,

"Sorry, are you in the band?!"

Your soul leaves your body.

Somewhere in the distance, the guitarist is signing an autograph. You nod, mumble something about needing to check your amp, and retreat into bassist obscurity.

If any of these lines have worked for you... please.
Report back immediately. Seriously. I need to know.

How You're Trying (and Failing) to Get Noticed

You've realized that blending in too much makes you practically invisible. So naturally, you tried to fix it. And, oh boy, you really tried...

First, you thought staying silent during rehearsals and gigs would make you seem mysterious - like a moody artist whose music does all the talking, the kind of guy who only speaks to drop profound one-liners between songs. Instead, everyone just assumed you forgot how to socialize. Even the sound guy didn't mistake you for deep - he just thought you were silently complaining about the mix.

Then came *'The Bass Face Era.'* You've seen the photos. Lips pursed, eyes half-closed, head tilted just enough to suggest you're either lost in the groove or fighting off a sinus infection.

You were going for soulful and immersed. Instead, it looked like you were holding in a sneeze or silently judging the audience's drink choices.

Still undeterred, you experimented with *'The Spin Move.'* You'd stayed up late bingeing live performances and thought, *'What if I just... spun around dramatically with my bass?'*

Technically, it worked. You spun. The audience noticed - mainly because you lost your balance and nearly wiped out the mic stand.

When that failed, you snapped.

Enough was enough - you went full *'Bass Hero.'*

Slapping. Popping. Tapping.

Running scales like your life depended on it, channeling the energy of every bass legend in history. Again, they noticed. But not the way you'd hoped. They weren't thinking,

'What a masterful performance!'

They were thinking,

'Why does the bassist look like he's battling his bass in an exorcism?'

So then you tried the opposite approach:

Pure, Silent Focus.

No smiles. No banter. Just you, the music, and a stare so intense it felt like you were questioning existence itself. Someone noticed. But instead of thinking,

'Wow, he's so deep',

they whispered,

"Is he... okay?"

And that's when it hit you... You were never meant to stand out. The singer can strut around like he owns the place, the guitarist can shred his way into the spotlight, and even the drummer - hidden behind an entire fortress of cymbals - somehow gets more attention than you. But you were never meant to be flashy. When you're locked in, the band is unstoppable. When you're gone? They crumble.

Maybe it's time to own the invisibility. While they chase the spotlight, you're the only one keeping the train from derailing.

Rare Social Wins:

When the Universe Accidentally Lets You Shine

Believe it or not, you've had your moments. Not many. But a few. Those rare, almost mythical instances when your existence as a bass player was acknowledged. These moments are so precious you still replay them every time you pick up your bass.

Like that one time - the legendary tone compliment. Someone noticed. Not your playing, of course. Just your tone. Still, it was enough to make your heart race. Flustered, you nodded, muttered something about "I've been tweaking the mids lately," and walked away before you could ruin it by talking too much.

Then, there was that unexpected moment. You were grooving, running a simple warm-up line when - clap...
Not out of politeness. A real clap. From someone. You couldn't tell where it came from, but it nearly made you stop playing. That single moment of stunned recognition? Still living off it. Possibly too much.

And, of course, the gear nerd encounters. Mid-set, as you anchored the groove with unshakable finesse, a guy in a vintage tour tee leaned in and yelled out: "What preamp are you running, man?"
Of course, you had no idea. You just nodded sagely and mumbled, "Vintage tubes, bro."
Whatever that means...

The unexpected soundcheck spotlight? The sound guy looked up. "Hey, can I get more bass in the mix?" For a second, you felt unstoppable - maybe even essential. You threw in a cheeky fill. Turns out, he was checking for buzz.

But the real highlight was that unexpected solo.
No one saw it coming. The guitarist's cable cut out mid-set.

One second, he was wailing away - the next? Nothing. Silence. And there you were, standing in the void. The audience stared. The band froze. You unleashed a slap line you'd been hoarding for months. For eight glorious seconds, you were the guy. Then the guitarist's cable crackled back to life, and he immediately drowned you out with a pentatonic shredding frenzy.

The singer's rare acknowledgment came out of nowhere. Mid-set, mid-song, mid-hair flip, he turned around and pointed straight at you.

"Give it up for the bassist, everybody!"

Your moment. Your spotlight. Was it because you nailed the groove? No. Your strap had broken mid-song, and you were now holding your bass at knee height, hunched over like a "human question mark," desperately trying to finish the chorus. Still counts.

Or it was that rare post-show validation? A random fellow musician - someone who knew their stuff - walked up, looked you in the eye, and said the holy words:

"Hey man... nice groove tonight."

You froze for a second. Was this honest - a genuine compliment? You just shrugged, keeping it casual.

"Oh, thanks. Just keeping it simple."

One night after a show, out of nowhere, the bartender walked over. You were exhausted. Coiling your cable for the third time because it kept tangling itself. He nodded and said,

"Hey, great set, man!"

You smiled. Finally, some recognition. But just as you tried to respond, he added,

"Can you move your stuff? I need to mop this area..."

These rare wins matter because they're proof - evidence that you can be noticed. That the world does hear you, when it's forced to. But imagine if you could get noticed without a gear malfunction, near-injury, or total silence.

The Sound Guy's Perspective:

No, He's Not Sabotaging You

Let's clear something up. The audio engineer - whether he's shaping your recordings in the studio or running live sound at your gigs - is not out to get you.

I know it feels personal. You're locked in, grooving, feeling the weight of your bass notes vibrating through your chest. And yet, somehow, in the grand sonic landscape of the mix... you're gone. Vanished. It's just a low-end whisper that nobody but you seems to notice.

You look over. He's behind the console, barely glancing up, lost in his board, twisting knobs like you're not even there. It feels deliberate - a calculated act of war. You could swear he just turned you down instead of up.

The truth is, you're not even on his radar enough for sabotage. To him, you're just another moving part in the swirling chaos of frequencies he's desperately trying to wrangle into something the audience can hear. He's got bigger fires to put out. A guitarist who's decided mid-show that his tone needs "just a little bit more presence." A singer who suddenly can't hear himself and requires "a touch" more reverb - only to complain ten seconds later that it's too much. A drummer pummeling his snare like it's responsible for all his life's problems, forcing the engineer to ride the faders like he's landing a plane in a thunderstorm.

Here's the thing about bass - it plays by different rules. You don't cut through like a guitar. You don't snap like a snare. You sit in the mix, creeping through the walls, rattling the floorboards, and subtly reshaping the entire room without most people even realizing it.

From your spot on stage, dialed into the groove, you feel like your tone is barely registering. But out in the audience, you're everywhere. The low-end frequencies don't just land in people's ears - they hit them. Wrap around them. Sink into their ribcages like an invisible force pressing against their chests. The sound guy hesitates when you ask for more bass because he knows what happens next. Turn you up too much, and suddenly, drinks are vibrating off tables. The guitarist starts complaining that his "mids are getting lost." The singer panics because he "can't feel the room anymore." The keys guy - who has remained completely silent through the process - quietly adjusts his pad volume until it dominates everything, drowning the entire set in an ethereal, cinematic atmosphere. And at that point, the sound guy has one mission: containment. You, my friend, are not being muted. You're being managed.

At some point, you did it. Walked up to the sound guy after soundcheck, pulling off your most serious, professional musician face, and said something like:

"Hey, man. Can you make my bass a little warmer? But also, like, punchy? And, you know... a bit darker?"

It felt like a valid request at the time. You were communicating a need. You didn't realize that you had just described every bass tone ever. He nods. He reaches for the board. He twists a knob. Did he change anything? Probably not. But he gave you a thumbs-up, enough to make you believe your tone was better. That's the game. Because let's be real - he's already EQ'd you exactly where you need to be. He's already battling a stage mix threatening to spiral into absolute anarchy. And he knows, with every fiber of his exhausted, underpaid soul, that your bass sounded fine the whole time.

It's easy to believe the sound guy is against you. But if he wanted to make your life miserable, he wouldn't just lower your bass in the mix but make people hear it... in the worst possible way. He'd crank the wrong frequencies, turn your punch into mud, and make your tone feel flabby and lifeless. He'd let the subs rumble just enough to be felt but never heard, leaving you frustrated while the audience wonders why their stomachs feel weird.

But he doesn't do that. Because, he wants you to sound good. A clean, punchy mix makes his job more manageable. He knows the reality - your bass is more than just a sound. It's a presence. A force. Something that moves the music forward even when nobody consciously registers it.

So, while you're agonizing over the difference between *vintage warmth* and *modern punch,* he's making sure the entire show doesn't collapse under the weight of competing egos and questionable tone decisions. And maybe, just maybe, that's the real reason he doesn't always have time to acknowledge your particular request for a "little more growl, but not too much." Because while you're locked in, shaping the groove, he's ensuring anyone can hear it at all. Which is kind of the point.

Audience Misperception:

What You Think vs. Reality

Ah, the audience. The final judges of your musical greatness. Or so you've told yourself.

In your mind, they're locked in. Feeling the groove. Swaying, hypnotized by your quiet mastery. You picture hushed whispers rippling through the crowd:

"Damn... that bassist! He's the heartbeat of this band. So understated. So smooth. Look at the way he barely moves. He is the music."

Half the crowd isn't even sure if you're playing. From their perspective, you're just there. A shadow off to the side. Steady. Still. Almost too still. If they notice you at all, it's only because you suddenly moved your left foot slightly - to hint that you're not a statue.

You're holding the groove. Keeping it all together. Yet no one's looking. The guitarist is balancing precariously on his pedalboard mid-solo, wearing a face that suggests spiritual awakening. The drummer is drenched in sweat - enough to hydrate the entire front row - hammering out a fill so long it could be its own separate track on the album. The singer is busy adding another scarf to his ever-growing collection while making weird bedroom eyes at the audience. The keys guy is barely moving, lost in his glowing fortress of synths - somehow still more noticeable than you. And you are locked in, holding it down. Playing a note so solid, so reliable, so unshakably steady... You might as well be waiting for a bus.

And then - you stop playing. That's when everything changes. The groove vanishes. Everything feels hollow. The guitarist stumbles, then suddenly riffs. The drummer falters, looking around like someone had triggered the fire alarm. Mid-scarf flip, the singer turns, eyebrows raised.

Because, dear bassist, you were the foundation all along. Do they realize it? Not really. But they feel it. You're why the music doesn't collapse into a swirling mess of feedback and ambition. You're the pulse, keeping it all from completely falling apart. And honestly, isn't that just badass?

The Bassist's Flowchart of Doom

A Guide to Whether or Not You're Getting Noticed on Stage

You've been asking yourself for a while now: Is this the night someone finally notices you? Let's break it down. Imagine a chaotic decision tree forming in your head, each step a twisted path through the unpredictable world of band life. Ready to navigate? Here we go:

Step 1: Are you playing your bass right now?
☑ **Yes!** Good start. Move to Step 2 - but double-check your tuning, just in case the guitarist "borrowed" your tuner again.
☒ **No?** Then why are you even holding it? Plug in before someone mistakes you for a stage tech. Then skip to Step 3 because you probably also skipped soundcheck.

Step 2: Can anyone hear you?
☐ **Yes...** Or are you just feeling the vibrations in your chest and fooling yourself again? If unsure, go to Step 5.
☒ **No?** Nudge your amp up - just enough to get noticed, but not enough to trigger the sound guy's death glare. Move to Step 4.

Step 3: Did you skip soundcheck?
☒ **Yes?** Bold move. Now you're stuck guessing if your tone is warm enough or if you're about to cause a minor earthquake. Move to Step 6.
☑ **No!** Nice. At least you're semi-professional. Go to Step 4.

Step 4: Is the audience reacting to your playing?
☑ **Yes?** Are they clapping because they love it - or because the song ended? Either way, move to Step 7.

☒ **No...** Give them time. Some audiences need years to grasp your genius fully. Go back to Step 2 and crank your amp slightly.

Step 5: Are you doing anything visually interesting?

☐ **Yes?** Did you spin? Honestly, did you almost take out the keys guy's rig again? Move to Step 9 and deal with the consequences.

☐ **No?** Try a subtle head nod - the "I'm deeply in the zone" look. If that fails, attempt Step 6 for redemption.

Step 6: Is the guitarist soloing?

☒ **Yes...** Congratulations, you're now officially invisible. Skip to Step 8 for damage control.

☑ **No?** That's a bonus. Weird. Should someone check if he's okay? Proceed to Step 7.

Step 7: Did the drummer just pull off an over-the-top fill?

☒ **Yes!** He's got the crowd - four shirts deep in sweat and still louder than your rig. Go back to Step 6 and rethink everything.

☑ **No?** This is your moment. Seize it - move to Step 10.

Step 8: Did the sound guy say, "You're too loud?!"

☑ **Yes?!** You've officially achieved the impossible. Take a moment to bask in that someone noticed your bass... even if it's for the wrong reason. Return to Step 4.

☒ **No...** He's too busy battling the guitarist's mids again. Accept your fate and proceed to Step 9.

Step 9: Did the sound guy make eye contact?

☒ **Yes?** Uh oh. Either you're asking for too much low-end, or you're out of tune. Go back to Step 3 and try not to panic.

☑ **No!** He's in survival mode, ignoring everyone until the gig ends. Proceed to Step 11.

Step 10: Are you playing a bass solo?!

☐ **Yes?!** Are you tasteful... or slapping your way through a ballad like you're auditioning for a funk festival? If it's the latter, skip to Step 12 for reflection.

☐ **No...** Probably for the best. Return to Step 2 to maintain your groove.

Step 11: Did the audience finally react?

☑ **Yes?** Oh wait... was it polite applause or just relief that the solo's over? Either way, move to Step 12.

☒ **No?!** Are you even plugged in?! Check your cable and jump to Step 5 for some visual flair.

Step 12: Did someone ask for more bass in the mix?

☑ **Yes!** You've ascended. Revel in the glory of being the heartbeat everyone forgot they needed. Finally, validation! Ride this high while it lasts, because next gig? You're back to Step 1.

☐ **No...** It's fine. They still felt it. Proceed to the Final Step.

Final Step: Did the set end?

☑ **Yes!** Well, you survived. Unless someone hands you another setlist - then welcome back to square one.

☒ **No?!** The guitarist's endless solo has outlasted everyone's patience. Proceed to unplug and prepare for the next inevitable battle quietly.

A Multiverse of Chaos

Congratulations! You've survived *The Bassist's Flowchart of Doom.* But the best part is that there are thousands of possible outcomes depending on how you answered. That's right - being a bassist is like starring in a "choose-your-own-adventure" book, except every ending somehow involves the sound guy glaring at you.

So, remember whether you nailed the groove or accepted silent defeat, the chaos is part of the gig. And somewhere in this vast universe of bass-playing possibilities, a version of you gets noticed. Probably.

Practice Exercise:

Explaining Your Role Without Sounding Like You're Begging for Validation

You've tried to explain your importance before. It probably went like this:

"Uh, yeah, I play bass... you know, the thing that holds everything together? No, I don't sing. No, I don't do solos. Well, okay, there was one solo, but it was tasteful. Look, all I'm saying is - if I stopped playing, this whole thing would fall apart, alright?!"

Did that sound convincing? No. It had the same energy as a tambourine player begging for more stage time. You deserve better - time to fix it.

So here's the challenge. Explain your importance without using the words *groove, vibe, glue,* or *foundation* - nothing you'd find in a hardware store.

Let's take it a step further - no metaphors that compare you to duct tape, scaffolding, or anything else that holds up a collapsing structure. Now, try again. Be bold. Unhinged. Slightly delusional but impossible to fact-check.

"The audience doesn't know it, but I hold their experience together."

See? Clean. Confident. Recklessly self-assured. And most importantly, so vague they can't argue with you. Because honestly, how would they even fact-check that? You can't measure "not sucking."

But if you want to lean in, go for something with impact:

"I am the unshakable force preventing this band from sounding like five malfunctioning metronomes battling for dominance."

Or

"The drummer plays like he's fighting off a swarm of bees.

The guitarist? Like he's throwing random notes at the wall just to see what sticks. I control the pulse of the universe."

Maybe even,

"Technically, I'm the only one in this band who knows what key we're in. But sure, let's trust the guitarist..."

If they still don't get it, let them experience a bassless version of their favorite song. Watch the groove vanish, the rhythm collapse and their soul wither.

And when you step on stage, don't just stand there blending into the shadows. Own the pocket. Play the note. Because the music doesn't just need a groove - it needs your groove. And if no one thanks you for holding it all together, hold them up anyway. They won't say it. But they'll feel it.

Now, repeat after me:

"I am the pulse. The backbone. The anchor."

"Not all notice the pulse - but they feel when it's gone"

"No more fedoras."

"No more fading into the background."

"I don't just play bass."

"I AM BASS..."

And it's about time the world recognized it.

Chapter 2

The Human Metronome

Loud, sweaty, and one broken stick away from a meltdown.

"For when others falter, you do not pause - you propel. Your glory is not found in restraint, nor is it hidden behind complex progressions, but instead it rings through the crash of cymbals and the rumble of toms, painting sound upon silence."

- The Faceless Guardian Of Time

The First Time You Hit Something That Mattered

Nobody picks up drums for nuance. No kid hears a song and thinks,
'*Wow, that ghost note in the pre-chorus really speaks to me.*'
No.
You picked up drums because they were loud. Because they were chaotic. Because guitars needed tuning, keyboards demanded theory, singers craved attention, and you just wanted to hit things.

That first time was pure, unfiltered mayhem. Beautiful. Untamed. Ear-splitting. You had no idea what you were doing, but it didn't matter. Sticks flew. Cymbals barely clung to their stands. Neighbors complained. Pets scattered. Parents regretted every decision that led to this moment. Siblings plotted your demise. Yet you didn't care - you were on a mission to turn raw chaos into something vaguely resembling rhythm.

After enough noise violations and family threats, you got your first real kit. Not a pristine, matching set - no, it was a Frankenstein rig of borrowed, pawn shop, and garage-sale parts, held together by sheer willpower and delusion.

The lie people outside the band believe is that drumming is "just hitting things." But without you, the band doesn't just lose rhythm - it loses momentum. The music slows, stumbles, and finally collapses. And yet, despite all that power, you're still the most ignored person on stage. Your kit is the loudest thing in the room. And you are right there in the middle of it. A blurry figure at the back, half-hidden by cymbals - noticed only in moments of disaster. It's a thankless grind. While they glide through the set with effortless cool, you're waging war against exhaustion, muscle cramps, and the slight suspicion that your lower back is about to file for separation. By the time the last note fades, they're basking in their rockstar glow, soaking in praise. You're wiping sweat off your snare, tracking down your stick bag, and wondering if drummers qualify for "hazard pay."

But you wouldn't trade it for anything. Because from the moment you first sat on that throne, you knew - *this wasn't just about playing drums*. It was about controlling the chaos and turning noise into movement, making *something bigger than sound*. And trust me, nobody does it better than you.

Loud as Hell, Yet Somehow Ignored

From behind the kit, you see it all - the crowd, the chaos, the slow-motion disasters waiting to unfold. You're the foundation and the failsafe - the only thing standing between a tight set and total collapse. And yet, nobody notices. Not when you speed up to save the dragging guitarist, throw in a fill to cover the singer's awkward pause, or subtly correct a bassist who has drifted away.

The second something feels off - half the room turns into rhythm scholars. And, to be fair, sometimes, it is your fault. Maybe you got cocky and threw in a tom roll that turned into an accidental drum solo. Perhaps you were too busy shooting a death glare at the sound guy to realize you were about to miss the downbeat. It happens. Still, without you, the whole thing falls apart in a heartbeat. Without rhythm, there's just noise. Given how some of your bandmates play, that line is already dangerously thin. Because drumming isn't just about keeping time, it's about herding egos in the moment. You're not just a musician but the only functional air traffic controller in a band of mid-air collisions.

The singer treats time like a vague suggestion - stretching syllables into new time zones, dragging notes like he's trying to outlast the measure itself. And when it all derails? Your fault. Apparently, the ability to count to four is your job now. Meanwhile, the lead guitarist operates on an entirely different wavelength. To him, the band is "just background noise for his personal sonic odyssey," bending time itself to accommodate whatever self-indulgent wailing he's up to. Despite having *rhythm* in his title, the rhythm guitarist hasn't heard about precision. Some nights, he's early. Some nights, he's late. Some nights, he somehow manages both in the same song.

Your closest ally in this warzone should be the bassist. In theory, at least, you're supposed to be a locked-in groove machine. But in practice, he's just off by enough to be maddening. When you sync up, it's magic... when you don't, guess who gets blamed.

And, of course, there's the keyboardist - existing in an entirely different spatial dimension. He's not thinking about rhythm. He's thinking about atmosphere, about layering, about *vibes*. He'll also complain your cymbals are "too harsh" - because drums are supposed to be subtle...

Floating above it all is the sound guy. The only one with actual control over what the audience hears. He listens to your kit for five seconds before deciding your toms are too boomy, your snare is too bright, and your kick drum "takes up too much space". Your floor tom has been erased from existence. He's already dialed it out of the mix like an act of revenge.

So you keep playing. Because if you stop, they'll finally hear how much of a mess it really is.

Flashes of Glory

Drummers don't expect applause. You're not the one screaming into a mic or shredding a solo. Your victories are rare and accidental - erased by the next crash before anyone even notices. But once in a while, the universe throws you a bone. And when it does, you cling to it like your last drumstick mid-solo.

Maybe it's that post-show moment.

"Hey, what kind of snare do you use?"

Your heart skips a beat. You brace yourself. You try to play it cool, nodding like it's no big deal. But inside, you're already rewriting your will to leave this person everything you own.

Then there's the perfect fill. Not planned and not overthought. Just one of those moments - hands faster than your brain, toms singing, snare exploding, the band locking in perfectly. The lead guitarist - yes, him - actually stops shredding long enough to shoot you *the nod.* A once-in-a-lifetime event. It's a moment worthy of its own documentary. And just when you think this is your time to shine, he steps on his wah pedal and buries you under another six-minute cry for attention.

And then, without warning, you're in the spotlight. The power cuts mid-song. Guitars vanish. The bass disappears. The venue hums with the flicker of fluorescent lights - the kind that never fully decides if it's on or off. Your kick drum starts thundering through the venue like a heartbeat in a horror movie. The crowd thinks it's part of the act. You think about taking a bow. Furious at being upstaged by a drum kit, the singer will never let this happen again.

Other times, it's about survival. A stick slips from your grip mid-roll. Time slows. Life flashes before your eyes. But instead of disaster, instinct takes over. Without missing a beat, you grab another stick and flip it. If the gods of rhythm feel generous, your rogue stick lands perfectly back in your hand. The audience is clueless. The band? None the wiser. And you? Absolute legend.

Then, there are moments where fate takes it further. Maybe, against all odds, the stick soars through the air. The audience gasps. As it drops, it smashes down on your crash cymbal in perfect time. The band is entirely unaware. You pretend it was intentional. But deep down, you know: *this is your peak.* You briefly consider quitting music altogether because it will never get any better than this.

But nothing beats the singer's utter dependence on you. He loses track of the song. Again. Turns. Eyes wide. Completely helpless. He doesn't know where he is. What comes next. How he even got here. His entire existence now rests in your hands. You throw in a cue fill, nudge him back on track, and watch as he triumphantly belts out the next verse like he meant to do that all along. He will never thank you. But deep down, he knows. And you see it in his panicked, sweaty eyes.

Then there are times when you wield a different kind of power. Maybe you hit the snare harder than usual - just to keep things interesting. Next thing you know... the crowd erupts into a pit. Was it you? Was it always going to happen?
Not that it matters. You're taking credit.

And when all else fails, you go out swinging. The band is out of songs. The singer is stalling, buying time with another awkward,
"You guys having a good time tonight?"
Pointless, yet effective.
The guitarist shrugs. The bassist is already zoned out. But the crowd isn't leaving. They're still chanting and waiting for more.So you make your move. Before anyone can think, you take matters into your own hands - literally.

A sudden, thunderous roll erupts from the toms. Sticks flying. Bass drum pounding like a war cry. The guitarist scrambles, fumbling to match whatever you just started. The bassist, startled awake, jumps in half a beat late - eyes wide, fingers guessing, confidence nowhere to be found. The crowd loses its mind.

For the first time ever, you started something. And for once, the drummer doesn't just keep time. He steals it.

Your Drum Solo Isn't Foreplay

Drumming is primal, sure - but let's get one thing straight. Keeping time at 200 BPM isn't a mating call. You might think dictating the pulse of an entire song translates into commanding admiration, but in the grand hierarchy of musical sex appeal, you rank somewhere between the triangle guy and the tour van's spare tire.

You've heard the myth "*Drummers have great rhythm - Rhythm is sexy.*" And you believed it. Somewhere in that crowd, someone must be watching - feeling the groove, locking eyes with you, thinking,

'That is a man who understands passion. That is a man who takes control.'

Except... they're not. They're watching the guitarist. Apparently, 'soul' and 'passion' aren't about rhythm - they're about mindless note stretching and guitar acrobatics.

Fine. Maybe rhythm alone isn't enough. Perhaps all you need is a statement - something undeniable. Something powerful. And that's when you make the mistake. You go for it - the drum solo. Guitarists use solos to look soulful, evocative, and tortured. Why not drummers? If done right, this could be your moment. And it is - just not the way you wanted. Drum solos don't scream mystery or depth. They scream,

"LOCAL MAN IN UNHINGED RAGE ATTACKS OWN DRUMS (FILMED IN 240P)."

You finish breathless, convinced you've just delivered a raw, thunderous display of primal musical seduction. The audience, however, is engaged in something far more pressing - checking their phones. Someone in the back just asked if mozzarella sticks are still half-price.

After the set, one soaks in the applause while another

dramatically replays their finest moment, lost in the glow of their own performance. And you're awkwardly searching for your stick bag, hoping - for once - someone will acknowledge that you just spent an hour keeping this entire circus from imploding. Maybe, if the universe shows mercy, someone walks by and mutters,

"Loved the fills, man. Thought the kit was gonna explode. Sick set."

And then vanishes into the crowd.

But, of course, that doesn't stop you from trying. You throw out a line after a gig, something low and steady, just enough weight to make it intriguing. Nothing.

You try again, and lean into its poetry. And still, no reaction. So you go all in, make it undeniable. A pause, a smirk - waiting for that flicker of recognition. And that's when she suddenly remembers she left her drink on another planet.

Not that you were expecting much. Rhythm is attractive - just not in the way you imagined. It's not the solos, sweat, or some elaborate display of technique. It's presence. How you hold your space, even from the back of the stage. The way you move, talk, and let the silence between words carry weight. That'll take you further than any double-kick pedal ever could. Just... maybe don't start a double-stroke roll demonstration over dinner. And just when you think it can't get any more humbling...

The Audience Thinks You Came With the Kit

The audience - those beer-clutching, rhythm-impaired enigmas - are the lifeblood of your gigs, but their grasp on drumming? Atrocious. They scream for the singer's high note; they worship the guitarist's solo, and as for you? You might as well be stage decor. At best, they acknowledge you. At worst, you're just another piece of stage equipment - sweaty and ignored.

Sure, you pretend it doesn't bother you. You tell yourself you're the backbone of the band, the unshakable force holding everything together. But deep down, just once, you'd like a little credit. Maybe even a compliment. Then some guy in a beer-stained band tee leans in, looks you dead in the eye, and says,

"Drumming looks easy."

Hold up. Wait a minute...

Drumming seems as easy as flying a plane when you're watching from the terminal. Out here, it's a full-body coordination marathon - controlling different rhythms with all four limbs while keeping a bunch of ego-fueled maniacs in check. But sure, go ahead - tell yourself you could totally do this if you "just practiced for a bit." Please. We'd all love to watch you crash and burn before you even figure out how to hold the sticks.

Then there's the assumption that you're just along for the ride, like a passenger on the band's journey to musical greatness. That would be fine - except the bus is on fire, the driver is asleep, and the bassist just leaned over and asked,

"Wait, what song is this?"

Your job isn't to sit back - it's to keep this whole thing from collapsing into a full-blown mess.

But the real insult is that some people don't even consider

you a real musician. No frets, no keys - just back there, flailing away like a raccoon in a dumpster, right? Never mind that your kick drum is the reason they feel the song in their chest or that your snare gives the chorus its punch. Never mind that they instinctively nod along to you - not the guitarist, lost in another quest for glory. But sure. Drumming isn't real music.

The one thing they might actually get right is that drummers are a little unhinged. And honestly, how could you not be? No sane person volunteers to be the only one in the band constantly burning calories on stage while everyone else barely breaks a sweat. You're battling exhaustion, gravity, and bandmates who treat tempo like a suggestion. And then there's the most infuriating assumption: that your only job is to *keep time.*

Right. That's like saying a chef's job is just heating a meal or a truck driver's job is just steering. Keeping time is the bare minimum. Your real job is controlling energy, shaping dynamics, and keeping everything tight - even when the band is actively making your life harder. You have to read their movements, anticipate disasters before they happen, and fix their mistakes without making it obvious. And that's the highlight. The audience may never scream your name, but they feel you. Every time their heads start nodding, every time they get lost in the groove, every time they move without thinking - that's you. They just don't realize it.

The Eternal Battle: Precision vs. Chaos

Drumming is a constant tug-of-war between two forces: precision and chaos. Lean too far into one, and you become a glorified drum machine - technically flawless but with all the thrill of a tax accountant. Give in to the other; you're less of a drummer and more of a liability. The trick is making everyone think you've got it under control. Or at least, that's what you want to make them believe.

Some drummers are precision overlords. Every hit is clockwork. The band depends on them, but nobody's excited. The guitarist keeps checking for hidden drum triggers. The bassist - for once - feels like the exciting one. Even the audience forgets them by song two.

Then there's the chaos enthusiast - the drummer who doesn't play the beat so much as wage war on it. Time signatures are loose suggestions. Fills appear without warning. That fast section in the middle? Now, twice as fast. The audience is on edge. The guitarist looks like he just saw a ghost. The bassist is secretly texting other bands. The singer is frozen in place, bracing for impact. Nobody knows what's happening anymore, but at least it's entertaining.

The best drummers live in the middle - tight enough to keep things from falling apart, unpredictable enough to keep things interesting. If you can hold the band together while throwing in just enough moments to make them wonder if they should be concerned - congratulations, you're doing it right. But whether you're a precision freak making music feel like a science project or a wild card keeping everyone in a mild state of panic, at the end of the day, you're still just the guy in the back hitting things for fun... and for a living.

And that brings us to another existential question:
Does size matter?

Your drum kit isn't just an instrument - it's a statement. A fortress. It is a reflection of your personality and, in some cases, your questionable financial decisions. Whether you stick to the essentials or construct a sprawling percussion empire, your setup tells the world exactly what kind of drummer you are. And no matter what you play, people will have opinions.

Some drummers keep it minimal - kick, snare, hi-hat, one tom, one crash. Clean. No frills. It says,
'*I play for the groove, not the gimmicks.*'
Respectable. But it comes with side effects. People assume you lost the rest of your kit in an accident. Someone - usually a guitarist - will ask, "Is that your warm-up kit?"
You force a smile, reminding yourself that at least you'll be packed up first.

Then there's the opposite approach - the drummer who looked at a basic setup and thought,
'*Needs more drums. More toms. More cymbals. A second bass drum. Maybe a gong - because why not?*'
It's an impressive display, but it comes at a cost. Specifically, an extra hour and a half of setup time, a lifetime of lower back pain, aching joints, and bandmates who conveniently disappear when it's time to load in.

Some drummers take it further. The vintage purist treats their kit like a sacred artifact. Every drum has a story. Every cymbal has been lovingly aged like fine wine. Modern drum manufacturing? Trash. New cymbals? Soulless.
The sound guy doesn't care, and the audience definitely isn't losing sleep over it. But when other drummers see you, they respect you. Until, of course, you start explaining in great detail why drum shells peaked in the late '70s.

Then there's the Frankenstein builder - part scavenger, part mad scientist. No two pieces match, but somehow, it works. Your kit is a chaotic masterpiece, assembled from pawn shops, Craigslist trades, and possibly an abandoned studio you weren't technically allowed in. Every gig is one missing drum key away from disaster, but you make it work through sheer stubbornness and prayer.

And finally, there's the hybrid innovator - half drummer, half NASA control centre operator. Your setup is an intricate blend of acoustic drums, electronic triggers, pads, and MIDI controllers. It's futuristic. Cutting-edge. Until your laptop crashes mid-set. And suddenly, you're just standing there, hoping nobody notices.

None of it actually matters. A great drummer can make magic with a three-piece kit, while a bad one can get lost behind a stadium-sized gear fortress. Whether rocking a stripped-down rig or sitting behind a monstrous wall of toms, the kit doesn't make the drummer. You do. Play like you mean it. Because at the end of the day, your kit isn't just gear - it's an extension of your style, chaos, and, let's be honest, your ego.

How to Survive Rehearsals Without Losing Your Mind

Rehearsals are supposed to be where a band tightens up, polishes the setlist, and functions like a cohesive unit. They're a migraine in musical form - equal parts chaos, passive-aggressive tuning battles, and existential dread.

It all starts with tempo - or rather, the lack of it. The guitarist plays 'by feel.' The singer waves their hands in some mystical attempt at counting in the band. The bassist? Waiting. Always waiting for someone else to take charge. That someone is you. So, you stomp out the tempo, loud and decisive, planting your rhythmic flag like a conqueror in uncharted territory. It helps occasionally, but more often than not, the guitarist stretches time to fit his solo, the bassist drags like he's stuck in another dimension, and the singer insists,

'*It feels fine to me.*'

Sure it does. Bring a metronome if you dare, but don't expect anyone else to love it. If all else fails, play louder. They'll fall in line - if only out of survival instinct.

For some reason, you're also the band's historian. The singer forgets the lyrics. The guitarist forgets chord changes. Someone always forgets the bridge. And when confusion hits, all eyes turn to you.

"You're the drummer - you should know this stuff!"

Oh, of course. While they're out there screwing up with confidence, you're juggling 16th-note fills, a double-time groove, and the occasional cymbal catch - but yeah, let's pretend your job also includes tracking their goldfish-level memory retention. At this point, bring a laminated cheat sheet. Chaos is not kind to paper.

And then there's the waiting. Rehearsals are 30% playing and 70% standing around while the guitarist tweaks his pedalboard for the hundredth time, the singer practices mid-song banter like they're hosting an awards show, and the bassist wanders off for another snack. You sit behind your kit, tapping rudiments on your thigh, praying someone says 'last run,' as a quick run-through drags into its second hour.

Speaking of snacks... Hunger is the silent killer of rehearsals. A 'hangry' bandmate is one missed beat away from a full-blown meltdown. You've seen it happen - a minor disagreement over the setlist spirals into an existential crisis, and suddenly, the guitarist is threatening to quit over a missing bag of chips. Always bring extra snacks. Deploy them strategically. Sometimes, a well-timed granola bar can defuse tension faster than a perfectly executed drum fill.

Despite the madness, rehearsals are where the magic happens - eventually. Sure, the singer throws scarves around, the guitarist disappears down a pedalboard rabbit hole, and the bassist glares at your fills, but somehow, it all comes together. You endure the chaos because the payoff - a tight, killer set - is worth it. Rehearsals don't have to be perfect, but they should be productive. End every session with a song that reminds everyone why they started this mess in the first place. It's the closest thing to harmony you'll get offstage.

The Soundcheck Chronicles:

Holding On Through Pre-Show Mayhem

Soundcheck should be a necessary but simple routine - a quick adjustment period to ensure everything sounds right before the show. In reality, it's a drawn-out exercise in frustration where you, the drummer, are simultaneously the most important and the least acknowledged person in the room. It starts predictably enough.

"Can I get the kick drum?"

You oblige, stomping out a steady beat, expecting this to end in seconds. But the sound guy squints at the board, turns a few knobs, and motions for more.

"Again."

You hit it.

"One more time."

Another thud. No feedback. There is no indication of progress. Just the sound guy adjusting sliders like he's defusing a bomb while your bandmates lose interest entirely. The guitarist is already rearranging his pedalboard - for no reason. The singer is scrolling through his phone. The bassist is somewhere in the void, lost in thought. Again.

Then comes The Great Cymbal Debate. The sound guy has a personal vendetta against your crash and ride, claiming they're too bright, too washy, and bleeding into every mic. He suggests you *'dial it back,'* as if you haven't already muted half your kit with gaffer tape. You give him a nod of agreement but change absolutely nothing.

Monitor mix negotiations are next. You ask for more kick. The bassist asks for less kick - because he apparently wants to feel nothing. The guitarist demands to hear himself above all else. The singer needs *'just a little more me,'* which, translated, means turning everyone else down to near silence. The sound guy sighs, adjusts the mix in a way that pleases no one and moves on.

And just when it seems like you're getting somewhere, gear malfunctions appear out of nowhere. Your hi-hat clutch mysteriously loosens itself. Your snare, which sounded perfect earlier, now has the tonal depth of a wet cardboard box. Your floor tom is resonating like a trash can in a windstorm. Every bandmate is looking at you like you personally sabotaged your own gear.

Through all this, the sound guy is your last line of defense. Annoy him, and your drums vanish from the mix. Play nice, and he might actually let the audience hear your snare. It's a delicate balance.

And whatever you do, don't smash your crash cymbal during sound check. He already thinks you're a problem - no need to confirm it.

Lock, Stock, and A Few Shattered Cymbals

Touring sounds like the dream - sold-out shows and pure chaos. In reality, it's a test designed to break drummers first - with physical labor, logistical nightmares, and the creeping realization that you should've picked harmonica instead.

It all starts with load-in. The guitarist strolls in with a single gig bag slung over his shoulder like he's embarking on an adventure quest. The singer casually carries a pristine microphone case - probably velvet, definitely purple. You're hauling an entire drum kit through the venue doors, sweating through your shirt before you've even touched a drumstick. Your bandmates look at your multiple trips and suddenly remember they need to check out the stage setup or grab a drink real quick. Some make a half-hearted attempt to help - lifting a stand, rolling in a floor tom - before conveniently vanishing. The bassist, who was right next to you a second ago, is now locked in a deep conversation with the sound guy about DI levels. The guitarist grabs one cymbal bag and immediately disappears into a vortex of fine-tuning his pedalboard for the soundcheck that hasn't even started yet. And the roadie? He's really just someone's best friend with a backstage pass. He puts in five minutes of effort, then magically reappears at the merch table, flirting with the merch girl. Again.

Then there's the van. If it doesn't break down halfway through the tour, that's a win. You wedge yourself between an amp and a tangled mess of cables that have somehow fused into a single entity over time. There's no legroom. The air is thick with stale snacks, body odor, and the unmistakable stench of cigarette smoke, courtesy of the one member who can't wait till the next rest stop and insists, "Don't worry, I'll blow it out the window."

Someone - always someone - has claimed an entire row for himself like a warlord defending his territory while the rest of you battle over inches of space.

Gas station stops offer brief moments of relief. Still, even those are a test of endurance: overpriced food, suspicious bathrooms, and the crushing realization that your drummer's cut of the tour profits will barely cover the coffee-and-muffin combo you just grabbed.

Once it's all done and dusted - the gig over - the night takes one of two paths. Some band members inevitably end up at a wild afterparty, waking up in a bed that most definitely wasn't assigned to them at check-in. Others collapse onto a motel mattress, watching TV at a responsible volume like a man twice their age. The following day, the van is a mix of sunglasses, hangovers, and quiet reflection as you prepare to do it all over again.

Gear malfunctions are inevitable. Drumheads split. Sticks snap. Cymbals shatter at the worst possible moment.

You've packed spares, but never enough. By night three, duct tape is the only thing holding your kit together. The snare sounds hollow, your throne wobbles like it has an agenda, and your hi-hat stand is betraying you in real-time.

And let's not forget backstage. If that word makes you think of luxury and relaxation, think again. It's usually a dimly lit storage closet with a single white plastic chair and a bathroom that hasn't had a functioning lock since day one. On the rare occasion, there's an actual green room, it's already been claimed - the singer is using it for pre-show focus, the guitarist has taken over the only couch for an emergency pedalboard adjustment. The bassist is missing, presumably lost in the venue's labyrinth of questionable hallways. You're standing awkwardly by the exit, guarding your stick bag, hoping for a moment of peace before the chaos begins.

But despite the sweat, exhaustion, and the overwhelming sense that your lower back may never recover, touring has its moments. The inside jokes that only happen when you're crammed in a van together for weeks. The adrenaline rush of a perfect set. The unexpected encore that makes you forget how little sleep you've had. The rare moment when you realize - between loading in and loading out - why you started doing this in the first place.

You don't get the glory, and you definitely don't get the lightest workload. But if touring is a war, you're in the trenches. And somehow, despite all of it, you keep coming back for more.

For the People at the Back

People struggle to describe what drummers do. They'll throw out vague compliments like,
"You've got great energy!" Or "Man, you really hit hard!"
Like you're an overly enthusiastic construction worker.
If they're feeling generous, they might add, "Dude, you must have insane cardio."
And that's about the level of recognition you get for keeping the ship from sinking, making sure everything doesn't drift entirely off course. And when someone finally asks what you do, they expect a neat little answer. Something humble. Something predictable. Something that makes sense to them.
But you don't settle for that. Instead, you drop lines like,
"I control time." Or "I turn chaos into movement."
Maybe even,
"Without me, this band is just a collection of egos guessing when to come in."
You don't need to explain it. They already feel it - even if they pretend they don't. Every great song they've ever loved? A drummer was behind the wheel. Every time they disappeared into a song? That was you. They don't think about it, but they feel it - in the kick, snare, and pulse that moves them. And that's the beauty of it.

While the singer preens and the guitarist fights for the spotlight, you don't beg for attention - you command it. You are the storm. The force that lifts a crowd off its feet or drops them into silence with one perfectly timed pause.

So when the dust settles, the last cymbal rings out, and the room exhales after the final note, you know exactly what you did. You didn't just keep time. You shaped it, you made it, and you made it unforgettable. And whether they realize it or not, they were all moving to your beat.

They always have been. It just hasn't hit them yet.

Chapter 3

The Shredder in the Spotlight

**Six strings, one giant ego,
and an amp that goes to eleven.**

"The loudest sound is not the note you play - it's the one you fight to hold back, lingering just beyond the strings."

- ***The Unsung Session Legend***

The Day You Discovered Noise Could Be Beautiful

It wasn't just music. It was a force. You were twelve, standing in the middle of a sweaty, overcrowded venue - probably too young to be there - clutching a flat soda as "Thunderstorm Overdrive" ripped into their set. And then you saw him...
The Guitarist. Tight neon strap. Oversized sunglasses. Hair sculpted by chaos itself. A solo bending every note, dripping in delay, shaking the venue while the drummer casually cracked open a beer mid-fill. The crowd was losing their minds. And you didn't just hear it - you felt it. Every chest-rattling note. Every reverberating riff cutting straight into your soul. This wasn't logic. It was instinct. And in that moment, you knew: you weren't just meant to listen to music. You were born to own it.

So you picked up a guitar. Not for balance. Not for subtlety. Because music wasn't loud enough, and you were here to change that. Every gig, every practice, every late-night jam session became a mission - not just to play but to move people the way the music had moved you. And then you started chasing it. Dialing in your pedalboard like a tone-obsessed lunatic, flooding solos with so much modulation, the sound guy questioned whether the mix was even possible. Every gig was another chance to prove you weren't just part of the sound. You were the sound.

But there's always another guitarist. And when there is, it's no longer a band - it's a battleground. The lead guitarist sees every note as an audition for guitar immortality. The rhythm guitarist strums like he believes three-chord progressions hold the key to enlightenment. And at that point, the bassist is just trying to survive the fallout. Because being a guitarist isn't just about playing music; it's about commanding attention - being the loudest thing in the room, even when the audience just wants to hear the song.

But here's the real question: Do they feel your sound - or just how loud you are? Let's find out.

You're Either Playing Too Little - Or Way Too Much

You remember the first time you picked up a guitar - the way your fingers curled around the neck, the feeling of endless possibilities. You weren't just learning an instrument. You were about to change music forever. Or so you thought.

At first, every riff felt like a masterpiece, and every solo was a direct transmission from the gods of rock. You played until your fingers ached, convinced that destiny was waiting to be discovered somewhere in the chaos of your bedroom amp. But then something shifted. It wasn't enough to play. You needed to be seen. The amp got louder. The solos got longer. One day, you even dragged a fog machine into rehearsal - because stage presence starts here. And this? This is where it gets dangerous. There's a fine line between commanding attention and refusing to let it go.

You start pushing it further. Maybe just a little louder or longer - just enough to leave an impression. The outro stretches into an extended jam, hanging long after the singer thanked the crowd. The solo lingers past its natural expiration date, dragging the song with it. It's not enough to be heard. You have to make sure they remember you.

The audience isn't lost in your masterpiece - they're just timing how long it'll take to get another drink. Your bandmates are already planning an intervention if you add one more pedal, and the sound guy's contemplating whether to turn up the singer or pretend to.

Loud doesn't mean legendary. Yes, the crowd feels the volume. But they'll remember not how many decibels you cranked - it's whether the music hit their hearts, not just their eardrums. Because sometimes, the real challenge isn't being heard. It's knowing when to step back. And that space between the notes? That's where the magic happens.

The Solo Obsession Spectrum

(Or When a Solo Overstays Its Welcome)

At first, you had restraint. A tasteful bend here, a subtle lick there - just enough to add flavor without hijacking the song. It was classy. The singer wasn't glaring at you. The bassist hadn't rolled his eyes yet. Even the sound guy, for once, left your fader alone. You were a team player.

Without realizing it, you started to lean in, stretching phrases, feeling the solo take shape beneath your fingers. One foot found its way onto the monitor. Your gaze lifted toward the middle distance as if the universe's secrets were being transmitted through your fretboard. In reality? You were recycling licks you'd played a hundred times before. But to you, this was poetry.

And then... the floodgates opened. Harmonic squeals. Rapid-fire tapping. Arpeggio sweeps because why not? Last night's YouTube rabbit hole had armed you with some very questionable techniques you could barely execute - but damn it, you were going to try. You weren't playing the song anymore. You were playing for legacy.

By the time you realized what was happening, it was too late. The solo had spiraled out of control - dive bombs, two-hand tapping, delay repeats stacking into oblivion. The singer had already wandered offstage. The bartender closed tabs. The sound guy, exhausted, mentally checked out. The drummer barely clung to the tempo. The dead-eyed bassist muttered, "Oh no, not again..."

Then there's the outro solo that refuses to end. The song is over, the singer is thanking the crowd, and the audience is clapping. But you're still going. The drummer has put his sticks down. The bassist is already wrapping his cable. And somehow, impossibly, you persist.

Or maybe it's the overcompensation solo that starts as damage control. You botch the intro riff. Instead of playing it cool, you panic and overcorrect, unleashing every scale you know in a frantic, meandering disaster. The audience isn't impressed. They're enduring it. Somewhere, the rhythm guitarist rolls his eyes, silently wishing this would end.

The truth is that the best solos aren't the longest or the flashiest. They're the ones that serve the song. Restraint matters. Space matters. If the audience checks their phones halfway through, you're not adding emotional depth - you're just dragging the song by its ankles.

So before you step up for that solo, ask yourself:
Are you playing for the music? Or just for yourself?
Because if your solo's dragging on longer than a drummer's stick twirl, it's not a masterpiece. It's a hostage situation.

Rhythm vs. Lead: A Battle of Egos

It's a rivalry as old as rock itself - the rhythm guitarist and the lead guitarist, locked in a never-ending turf war no one else in the band understands or bothers to mediate.

The rhythm guitarist sees himself as the backbone, while the lead drifts into high-gain daydreams, chasing glory on a fevered whim. Without him, the song falls apart. His power chords are the glue. His strumming is the bedrock. His consistency makes the whole thing sound like actual music instead of a Guitar Center on Black Friday.

And yet, every time the rhythm guitarist finds his groove, Captain Endless Solo swoops in, hijacking the track like he's trying out for the next Guitar Hero sequel. The moment he starts feeling tight and locked in, the lead guitarist sees an opportunity. Why let an excellent rhythm section go to waste when he could soar over it with a spontaneous, 32-bar, harmonic, squeal-filled showcase of ego?

The lead guitarist has his own version of reality. Sure, rhythm is essential - but, honestly, no one is air-guitaring to a G chord. People came for the solos, the sweeps, the bends, the moments of raw, fretboard-melting genius that should bring tears to their eyes. Or at least would have... if they were actually paying attention. The rhythm guitarist sees himself as the backbone. The lead? He sees him as a necessary evil - a stepping stone on the way to greatness.

While they battle for dominance, the rest of the band is left to pick up the pieces. The bassist, exasperated, knows no one will even notice if he goes silent. The drummer, exhausted, wonders how many more of these battles he can survive before he snaps. The keyboardist sighs, knowing his input only matters when the sound goes sideways. And the singer is planning his next move, which probably involves sabotaging the guitarists in the most subtle way possible.

But in the end, none of it matters. The decision has already been made. The sound guy - calm, calculated, and three beers deep - has already taken control. The mids have been cut. The solos have been turned down. The vocals have been cranked to avoid a riot. Because at the end of the day, no one - not the crowd, not the band, and definitely not the sound guy - wants to sit through a six-minute bridge dispute disguised as a jam session.

The Sound Guy vs. Your Delusions of Volume

You think of him as the enemy - the gatekeeper standing between your masterpiece and the audience, the one dialing your amp from arena-level thunder to background jazz quartet with a single twist of a fader. You don't trust him. He doesn't get your sound - the delay-soaked, mid-boosted, reverb-drenched masterpiece you've meticulously sculpted with twelve pedals, two amps, and a dream. You assume he's strangling your tone out of spite. Or jealousy.

At the console, he watches the chaos unfold,
"Oh great, here we go again..."
He announces to no one in particular. This isn't new. It isn't even the worst case. This is just another entry in the long, exhausting record of guitarists who believe louder means better and refuse to accept that their 100-watt half-stack already triggers seismic activity three towns over.

And the war begins. It starts subtle - just a little volume bump so your tone "cuts through." The rhythm guitarist panics and retaliates with his own boost. The bassist, now functionally mute, attempts diplomacy. "Guys, maybe we could..."
But before he can finish, the lead guitarist has launched into another solo - swirling and soaring. No one asked for it. Nobody can stop it. The rhythm guitarist responds with a wall of overdriven chords, each one screaming,
"Hey, I'm here too!"
Unable to hear anything, the drummer starts playing like he's fighting for his life. The singer vanishes into the noise, barely heard over the chaos. At this point, the sound guy has one goal: containment. That's why, when you shoot him a death glare mid-set and motion for more guitar in the mix, he just nods... and pretends to turn a knob.

Because, in reality, he's already dialed your amp down twice, and the only reason the crowd can still hear the singer is because he's practically screaming for his life.

But of course, you are different. Your sound needs to be heard, right? That's what the last fifty guitarists thought, too. And as the sound guy subtly lowers your volume one last time, he's not trying to ruin your life - he's saving the audience from permanent hearing damage and making sure the bassist doesn't snap and strangle you with his patch cable. If your amp is loud enough to rattle beer glasses off the bar, you are not a genius. You are a structural threat.

Gear vs. The Quest for Perfect Tone

It started small - a beginner's amp, a secondhand distortion pedal, and the naïve belief that one magic combination would unlock your signature sound. Fast-forward a few years, and now you're standing in the middle of a pedalboard jungle, surrounded by boutique overdrives, experimental fuzzes, and three "vintage" reverb units, none of which are actually vintage. Your gear isn't just a tool anymore. It's a lifestyle. A philosophy. A never-ending pilgrimage toward the Holy Grail of Tone.

At first, it was innocent. Your first amp was a choice made with purpose - the same model your hero used. Plugging in felt like summoning their ghost. But when your playing didn't suddenly sound like theirs, the problem couldn't be you.

No, no - it had to be the amp. Maybe it needed a better speaker. Perhaps a different cab. Maybe a boost pedal to push it just right. And so, the quest began. A distortion pedal was the first addition - because everyone needs a little extra edge. Then, there was a delay because repeats meant emotional depth. Then another delay because the first one wasn't quite warm enough. Then, there was an overdrive different from the one you already had. Before you knew it, your pedalboard had mutated into a blinking, tangled monument to overthinking. Setting up for a gig became a logistical operation. A single loose cable could derail your entire existence.

But no matter how much gear you stacked, the imperfections never disappeared. The overdrive wasn't quite right, the chorus lacked depth, and the delay was too cold. The answer, of course, was simple: buy more gear. If one fuzz pedal wasn't quite right? Get two. If one delay didn't capture the feeling in your soul? Stack three of them. Were you even playing if you weren't drowning in an overdrive stack so thick it sounded like molten lava?

And this is where it happens - the moment when gear obsession stops being about tone and starts being about identity. You weren't just a guitarist anymore. You were a tone sculptor - a seeker of sound. At least, that's what you told yourself as you passionately explained true bypass vs. buffered signal paths to someone who did not ask.

Meanwhile, the bassist idly scrolled through his phone, waiting for the set to start. The drummer sighed, tapping mindlessly on his snare. The sound guy, already exhausted from soundcheck, watched silently as you tweaked the same pedal setting for the fifth time, wondering how much he was getting paid for this.

The audience didn't care if your overdrive was boutique or bargain-bin. They just wanted you to stop and play something that resembled the song. They weren't listening for the subtle difference between germanium and silicon diodes. They just wanted you to stop fiddling with knobs and play something before they lost interest entirely.

Eventually, the breakthrough hits: gear is a tool, not a crutch. The right fuzz pedal might make you feel invincible, but it's not what makes you a great player. No matter how many boutique pedals you stack or how many amps you own, the real test is simple: What happens when the gear is stripped away? Because the magic isn't in the pedals. It's in the hands of the player.

And seriously - leave the fog machine at home. Nobody wants another smoky soundcheck.

The Art of Overdoing It

You'd seen it before - the move. The mid-solo spin, the effortless stage command, the kind of thing they replay in slow motion in a music documentary. It looked iconic. You figured it was time to try it. Except the second you went for it, your strap locked up, your guitar yanked like a stubborn seatbelt, and suddenly, you weren't spinning - you were fighting for survival. The bassist barely ducked in time. The mic stand didn't. And the crowd? Watching you desperately untangle yourself before the song ended.

And that wasn't even the worst of it. Things spiraled somewhere between your pedal obsession and the unfortunate belief that hurling yourself across the stage like a human cannonball would electrify the audience. You weren't moving the crowd - you were just moving too much.

Then came the shirtless phase. In your mind, it was a legendary rock 'n' roll moment. In reality, you looked like a guy who wandered onto the stage in the middle of a yoga class - posture wrecked, sweat pouring, string bends wobbling like they weren't sure they wanted to be there. The only thing melting faces was secondhand embarrassment. But if there's one thing you still wince about, it's the solo. The one where you went for a pinch harmonic, aiming for that high-pitched scream that makes an entire stadium explode. Instead, it came out somewhere between a dying seagull and a chainsaw in distress. The audience didn't cheer. They just clenched their teeth and braced for impact. You pictured them in awe, leaning in, eyes closed, hanging on every bend, every squeal. You weren't just playing - you were reshaping reality, bending sound to your will. But in reality? Not so much.

Over by the bar, a group was glued to their phones. In the corner, a couple debated whether to get nachos or wings. The guy in the front row squinted, trying to figure out if you were still on the same song - or if you'd gone rogue. By minute five of your solo, they weren't lost in your playing - they were just counting down the seconds until the next song. You were up there, channeling raw emotion, lost in the moment. The crowd saw a sweaty guy hunched over his pedalboard, face twisted in something between agony and confusion. And as for the sound? To you, it was a pristine symphony of tone, the culmination of years of practice. To them, it was a relentless wall of screeches and squawks - whatever emotional depth existed drowned in a sea of distortion.

It's not about playing louder, faster, or longer. Maybe - just maybe - cut the fourth solo. Let the song breathe for once. And for the love of all things sacred, ease up on the swirling modulation before it starts to sound like you're broadcasting from a haunted funhouse.

Overcompensating doesn't make you a legend. It makes you a cautionary tale. The audience doesn't care about your gear, your spins, or how much sweat you left behind. They only remember how you made them feel.

And by 'feel,' I don't mean tinnitus...

Flirting in Drop D: A Masterclass in Failure

You didn't just pick up the guitar to play music. Deep down, you knew it was more than an instrument. It was power. Loud, raw, untamed power. And, if we're being honest, you thought it might make you irresistible.

You pictured yourself center stage, clothes clinging, hands shaking, heart still racing, fingers flying across the fretboard, while she stood mesmerized in the crowd. The solo would hit, and the world would fade away. Just you, the music, and the unshakable certainty that this moment - this very note - would leave an imprint on her soul.

Then reality kicks in. She's not watching your solo. She's wondering what time the gig ends. That 12-minute shred session you thought was dripping with passion sounded more like a frantic, out-of-tune siren wailing in the distance. The moody, eyes-closed, back-to-the-crowd stance? Less tortured artist, more guy who just remembered he left the stove on at home. That lightning-fast flurry of notes - the one you thought would leave her breathless - just left your hand cramping while the rest of the band silently begged you to wrap it up.

Still, you persist. Words may help. You may need to show her the depth of your musicianship. So you lean in, all drama and mystery.

"Want me to make my guitar cry?"

Except instead of a tasteful, bluesy bend, your hand slips, and the string lets out a dying mosquito whimper that neither of you can ignore. She shifts in place, eyes scanning for an escape.

You try again - pivot to theory.

"Mixolydian? No? Great, here's a 45-minute crash course."

Nothing makes hearts race like an unsolicited lecture on

modes. If she hasn't walked away yet, you double down.
"You like delay? Because I'm still repeating myself."
At this point, desperation sets in.
"I shred... emotionally."
Which, let's be honest, means you wrestle the fretboard like it personally offended you.
Or maybe you lean into sheer confusion:
"Ever wondered what harmonic dissonance feels like? No? Want me to show you anyway?"
The answer is no. Always no.

And just when you think you've hit rock bottom, you deliver the final, gasping attempt:
"I bring the soul of the music. The guitarist is the song."
By then, she's already gravitating toward the bassist.

The good news is that you've got stage presence. The bad? That's not the same thing as actual charisma.

You Can't Describe Fire - You Just Set It Loose

There were flashes - unplanned, unrepeatable - where your guitar really did steal the moment, for reasons other than sheer volume. They weren't part of some grand performance strategy. But for a split second, you almost felt like the hero you always imagined in your head.

Like that one time, the crowd actually cheered during a solo. Technically, it was soundcheck, and it might've just been the drummer's cousin being polite, but validation is validation. Or that moment when instinct took over, and you nailed the perfect power stance - one foot up on the monitor, neck angled, channeling pure sonic energy. right up until you tripped over your patch cable and unplugged yourself.

Then there was the post-show encounter when a fan casually said,

"Nice solos, dude."

Simple. Courteous. But you spent the entire drive home analyzing their tone, replaying the moment, wondering if it was genuine - or just a filler while they waited for the bathroom.

And let's not forget the time the rhythm guitarist completely botched the intro to the ballad, forcing you to step in and save the whole song with a graceful fill while he panicked. Did anyone thank you? Of course not. But you felt the silent respect. Yet again.

These were the moments, the tiny victories that reminded you why you started in the first place. You've spent years shaping your sound - tweaking your tone, chasing the perfect sustain, and dialing in that sweet spot between power and clarity. You've sunk more hours into reverb decay than most people spend on relationships. And yet, when someone asks what you play, you hesitate. You could say "guitar." You could talk about your rig, your pedal chain, your impeccable vibrato. But no words could ever do it justice. Because your role isn't something you explain - it's something you unleash.

A riff can turn an empty room electric. A single note, held just right, can tear a hole through time. When the moment demands power, movement, chaos - you're the one who delivers it. The one who makes it impossible to stand still.

They don't always understand what you do. Some think you're showing off. Others just hear the volume. But you're here for something bigger - more than approval, decibels, or solos-per-minute. You play because you can't help it. The fire doesn't ask permission before it burns. And when it's gone? Everything turns cold.

Chapter 4

The Alchemist of Airwaves

A Sonic Architect Lost in His Own World

"Yours is not the hand that leads, nor is it the voice that commands. You do not crave the roar of the crowd - you build the space where it belongs.

And though they may never say your name, when the sound fades and the stage feels hollow, they will know. You were there. You always were."

- The Architect of Echoes

The Day You Discovered the Keys

And Nothing Else Mattered

It started with a sound. Not a power chord. Not a drum fill. Just a single, shimmering note hanging in the air. Pure, endless, stretching beyond the room. It wasn't loud. It wasn't aggressive. But it shifted something. The space, the moment - the atmosphere itself. Other instruments played notes. This one created worlds.

While your friends hacked through their first "Back in Black" riffs, you were lost in something deeper. Textures, layers, the raw science of tone. They wanted to make noise. You wanted to shape the resonance around them. Your first keyboard was either a childhood relic, a yard sale rescue, or a cursed budget Casio with built-in demo songs. It didn't matter what it was. What mattered was that sound that made life stop for a second. The one that pulled you under like a riptide, drowning out everything else.

They laughed at you. Guitars had attitude. Drums had power. You sat alone with headphones on, twisting knobs, chasing something they couldn't feel. You weren't just playing an instrument. You were unraveling a universe of music. As they fought for lead spots, you were hunched over keys, lost in the swirl of reverb tails and delay feedback. They posed in the mirror; you sculpted soundscapes. And sure, they dismissed it. They didn't get it. Not yet.

But then came the moment. The first time you sat in with a band. The first time you added a single pad that *changed* the song. The first time someone turned to you - eyes wide - and said, "Whoa... that sounds sick."

That's when it all clicked. You had no idea what kind of battle you were walking into. But none of that mattered. And that sound? It still gives you chills.

The Battle for Sonic Space

There's only so much space in the mix. A delicate balance where every instrument should, in theory, coexist peacefully. That is until the guitarist arrives. To him, all space is his space. Every frequency, every decibel, every inch of sonic real estate belongs to his beloved amp. He does not sit in the mix. He is the mix. And you're just some button-pressing squatter taking up valuable lead tone territory.

At first, you're hopeful. Maybe there's a way to coexist.

"Let's balance our EQs," you suggest.

He nods. Thinks about it. Then, he cranks his amp and erases you from existence. Chords? "Muddy." Melodies? "Too much." Synths?

"Dude, this isn't *Stranger Things*..."

An organ swell? He instinctively turns up louder, just in case. So you adapt. Creeping into frequencies so high or low he doesn't even notice, you slide under the radar. You sneak in subtle pads during quiet moments to fill the space - just enough to feel present without setting off alarms. It seems like you've found a way to survive for a while until he notices and drowns you out completely. Because in his mind, the only thing worse than a keyboardist... is a keyboardist people can actually hear.

So little by little, you fade. You let him rule his kingdom. Then one day, something shifts. The sound feels thin. The guitarist stops mid-solo, the singer looks around, the drummer hesitates. A quiet realization dawns.

"Hey, can you add, like... something?"

And just like that, you're necessary again. Until the next solo.

Existing Just Outside the Spotlight

You are in the band. You are on the stage. You are, without question, making sound. But are you really there?

The guitarist gets his solos. The singer commands attention. Even the bassist, for all his subtle suffering, gets some acknowledgment. And the drummer? Loud, but oddly overlooked.

Off in the shadows, you're wrapped in a fortress of keys, buttons, and cables - necessary, yet invisible. It's not that they don't appreciate you. It's that they don't think about you. Your playing is so seamless that it goes unnoticed - until it's gone.

'Something sounds off. Why does it feel so empty? Oh wait, is the keyboard even on?'

You hit a single chord, and suddenly, the missing frequencies flood back in. The singer exhales in relief. The guitarist goes back to pretending he's in a sold-out stadium. The drummer gives a single, sarcastic thumbs-up. The bassist slowly turns away, not out of protest - just because he's never been that invested.

Your stage position says it all - tucked in a corner, half-hidden behind amps, drums, and an inexplicably large pedalboard. Strategically placed where your existence won't interfere with hair flips, stick tosses, guitar god theatrics, or the bassist's slow, unexplained migration toward stage left - grooving, bored, possibly looking for snacks.

From the audience's perspective, you could be a session player, the band's sound tech, or just some guy who wandered onstage and never left. Every now and then, someone scans your setup with mild curiosity.

"Wow, that looks complicated."

You nod. Waiting. Hoping. Maybe this time.

'Dude, that solo was insane!'
They weren't even looking at you.

This one time, everything fell apart. A synth pad vanished mid-chorus. A backing track glitched. One wrong note - and suddenly, the singer whipped around in panic. The guitarist looked at you for the first time all night. The bassist sighed dramatically, even though he had no idea what just happened. The drummer stayed oblivious - but only because he was already off-time. You didn't say a word. You fixed it. And they carried on, blissfully unaware you'd just saved the set from imploding. But that's fine.

You were never in this for the spotlight. While they fight to be heard, you're out here sculpting sound itself. Let them chase the attention. You've got frequencies to shape.

The Social Mirage

In a band, the hierarchy of attention is painfully clear.
The singer commands the spotlight. The guitarist basks in praise. Even the drummer - feral, sweat-drenched, and possibly concussed - somehow attracts admirers. And then there's you. The keyboardist. No mystique, no rebellious edge, no quiet air of danger. Nobody looks at you and thinks, *'This guy lives on the edge.'*
If anything, they assume you're just there to help with the sound or fill out the mix.

If the after-show scene were a battlefield, the singer and guitarist would soak in glory while you stand off to the side, holding someone's drink... Literally. You're not the guy they flock to. You're the one they trust to hold their drink while they flirt with the bassist. When someone notices, it's never because they're impressed.
"Wait, are you really playing that live? I thought it was a backing track."

Every once in a while, someone makes actual eye contact and asks what kind of keyboard you play. You brace yourself, ready for a real conversation about gear, tone, something that matters. And then:
"Oh cool. So, do you, like... control the lights too?"
And just like that, you remember your place.

One thing is certain: You don't need to be the center of attention. You've got sound design to perfect, new synth patches to build, and an entire sonic universe to manipulate. Let the others fight for dominance - you'll be over here, untouched by the chaos, finishing your drink while quietly adjusting a filter cutoff. Because while they chase fleeting admiration, you've got real work to do.

Just Here For The Synths

You already know how it usually goes. But every now and then, somewhere between the last note of the set and the first sip of your post-show drink, the thought creeps in:
'Maybe tonight's different...'
Just once, someone might see past the singer's theatrics and the guitarist's solos and recognize the quiet force behind the keys. Someone might finally realize that it's you who shaped the sound of the night, you who built the atmosphere from airwaves and intention.

It's not that you need validation. You've got synth patches to perfect, DAW projects piling up, and a home studio that could keep you busy for months - unless, of course, that dream synth you've been waiting years for finally drops. In that case, cancel everything. You'll be busy tweaking knobs and sliding faders like it's a religious experience. Anyway, back to the story. Let's face it, everyone craves a little connection now and then. So, against your better judgment, you take a shot.

The scene is set: dim lighting, post-show buzz, a perfect blend of casual and mysterious. You lean against the bar, fingers drumming absently on the counter, sipping your drink, exuding quiet confidence. When the moment feels right, you go for it. A simple line. Nothing desperate. Just something to spark a conversation - something that might, at last, make someone realize the keyboardist isn't just some tech guy filling in the gaps. And then, reality slaps you hard.
"So, did you enjoy the show?"
A safe, low-risk opener. If they were paying attention, it should at least get something going.
"Oh yeah! The singer was incredible!"
You nod, pretending that didn't sting.

Maybe a different approach.

"I can play you something beautiful right now."

It's not a pick-up attempt - just an offer to share a little of your world. A hint of mystery. A subtle flex. You sip your drink. Keep it moving.

"You should check out my home studio sometime."

A slow blink. A forced smile. You weren't flirting - you were inviting them into the one place you still feel in control. A glimpse into your universe where music isn't just played - it's built.

"Oh... uh... cool. Anyway, I should find my friends."

Even you admit - this is going poorly. You try once more.

"That last song? I wrote most of the chords."

They stare, confused.

"Oh! I thought the guitarist wrote everything?"

The betrayal burns deeper than it should. And that's the moment - the one where you realize, once again, you've lost to a guy who still thinks the pentatonic scale is the peak of musical theory. You could try again, lean in with one last effort, and throw in something about how you can build an entire song from scratch in real-time, but you already know where that road leads... *'Oh yeah! I actually dated a DJ once.'*

You finish your drink quickly. The conversation fades. Somewhere in the background, the singer is charming his way into someone's night. The guitarist is soaking up compliments. The drummer is still loudly explaining why the sound guy ruined his set. And the bassist - well, he disappeared an hour ago.

And just as you're about to head out, someone turns to you and asks, smiling:

"Hey, do you know the sound guy?"

You don't even answer. Just a slow nod, a quiet smirk, and a smooth exit before the conversation can get any worse. After all, you've got a new synth waiting at home.

The Subtle Art of Failing with Style

Some musicians step on stage and command attention without even trying. The guitarist launches into a solo, and people lose their minds. The singer barely exhales, and the crowd swoons. Even the drummer - sweaty, half-hidden - gets a cheer for twirling a stick or standing too fast. And then there's you.

You don't just want to be noticed - you try. Harder than you'd like to admit. But every time you reach for the spotlight, it dodges you like a well-rehearsed avoidance technique. The universe has already decided: you are not meant to be seen. Still, you refuse to accept it.

You get your moment - a synth solo, something dramatic, something undeniable. Your fingers fly, weaving melodies that would make Vangelis proud. The sustain stretches, the sound soars, the whole room should be feeling this. But before the final note even resolves, he's already stomping on his distortion pedal, launching into another shameless flex. No reaction from the crowd. No acknowledgment from the band. Nothing. Like a tree falling in a forest full of guitarists, you start to wonder if you even made a sound.

You may need to stand out more. You try something bold. A long leather coat, some dramatic eyeliner, a wide brimmed hat you're not sure you can pull off, and the quiet belief you now radiate mystery. You walk onto the stage feeling different. Elevated. A force to be reckoned with.

After the set, someone finally approaches. Your heart pounds.

"Dude, what was up with the hat?"

Not 'great playing.' Not 'loved your energy.' Just a single, stupid question about a foolish hat.

You try something else. Maybe movement. The singer

never stands still, the guitarist does that thing where he bends his knees and looks like he's discovering blues for the first time, the drummer is in a constant state of near-collapse - but you? You stand there. Focused. Stationary. Boring.

Not tonight. Tonight, you move. You throw yourself into it, bending over the keys dramatically, throwing a hand in the air for emphasis, maybe even attempting a little headbang. It doesn't help. Nobody notices - except for the guitarist, who gives you a weird look, and the drummer, who laughs mid-fill and almost drops a stick. So you go even bigger. You step to the mic. If the singer can command the audience, maybe you can, too. You clear your throat, channel every frontman you've ever seen, and...

"Let me hear you make some noise!"

Silence. A few people glance up, confused. Someone in the back asks their friend if the venue serves deep-fried pickles. The guitarist outright snickers. You slowly back away from the mic, making an unspoken vow: Never again.

And yet, somehow, nothing is worse than actually getting noticed. After the set, someone approaches. It's rare. Unexpected. But there they are - someone who saw you. Someone who got it. Almost.

"Whatever you were doing up there... it worked. You added something. Like - aaah - I can't explain it."

You smile, ready to bask in this moment - and immediately ruin it.

"Yeah, I was running a Prophet Rev2 for that warm sound, but I had some latency issues with my controller, so I had to manually compensate in real-time"

They're already walking away.

You are alone again. Maybe that's the real curse of being a keyboardist. It's not just that people ignore you - it's that the second they do notice, you somehow make it worse. And yet, for all of this, you don't stop. You keep trying. Because deep down, even though you know you'll never be the one getting the glory, you also know this: the moment the music feels empty - the moment something sounds off - that's when they finally notice. Not when you're there. When you're not.

The Band's Reluctant Tech Guy

At some point, you made a fatal mistake: you fixed something. It wasn't much at first - a buzzing pedalboard, a loose cable, a glitchy track. But that was all it took. You're no longer just the keys guy; you've become the band's go-to tech support, and that's not a position you can back out of.

It started innocently. But now, every technical problem, whether it's your responsibility or not, is yours to handle. The guitarist can't figure out why his tone sounds off, and the bassist's amp mysteriously cuts out mid-set. The drummer's track won't play, and the singer suddenly obsesses over his mic like you're the only one who can help.

And there you are, knee-deep in cables and connectors, desperately trying to keep everything from falling apart. You weren't asked to be the tech guy, but here you are, doing it anyway. You wish someone else would pick up the slack, but they don't. Not because they don't appreciate you - because they've just accepted that you know how to fix it.

By the time the show starts, you're already drained. But do they thank you? Do they notice that the show almost derailed before it even began? Of course not. The guitarist rips into his solo, convinced he's why everything sounds perfect. The bassist nods along, blissfully unaware he was just seconds away from total silence. The singer is still fussing with his mic. You remain invisible - still making sure they can take all the credit. You don't complain. You never do. Because deep down, you know the truth: if you don't fix it, nobody else will.

The Gear Spiral: How You Became a Synth Hoarder

At first, you just wanted a richer sound. A second keyboard, maybe a MIDI controller - just a few more tools. But somewhere along the way, it stopped being about improving your sound. It became an obsession.

Your room, once just a place to work, had slowly transformed. Cables cluttered every surface. Blinking LEDs lit the corners. Keyboards stacked against drum machines, samplers, and audio interfaces. Suddenly, you started designing stands and modifying desks, fitting more gear on top of each other until your workspace looked like mission control for a synth-obsessed space station. This wasn't about playing music anymore. You were crafting soundscapes, designing your art - one knob at a time. What began with a backup synth for live shows quickly escalated. You found yourself needing an analog piece to capture the warmth digital gear couldn't replicate.

Then came the vintage synth - the one you couldn't pass up - because they don't make 'em like that anymore. And just like that, it wasn't just about the keyboards. You had expanded into a full-blown sound laboratory.

It didn't stop there. Drum machines, samplers, and effect pedals made their way in. And when you realized you could make a modular rack work with your setup, it felt like the perfect addition. This was no longer just music. You were building sonic worlds - your own creative universe.

Naturally, your bandmates were confused.

"Didn't you just get a new synth? Why do you need another?" The guitarist asked, puzzled.

"How many of these do you need?"

The bassist wondered, watching in disbelief as you made space for even more gear.

"Uh, I don't even know what half of this stuff does," the drummer mumbled, his attention already fading. "And, like... do you press buttons, or does it play itself?" The singer asked, completely lost in the complexity of your setup. They didn't understand. They couldn't hear what you heard. You feel every change - the way a filter sweep shifts the mood of a song, the subfrequencies that add weight, the reverb that sits just perfectly in the mix. What they saw as unnecessary clutter, you saw as the tools of your craft. When they mock your hours spent fine-tuning, you don't respond. Instead, you turn the knob, adjust the filter, and let the sound bloom, filling the space until it almost vibrates the walls. At that moment, the room finally gets it. They stop talking. The music isn't just heard - it's felt. This isn't just gear. It's not a hobby. It's the pulse of everything that keeps you connected to the music.

More Than Keys

It all begins before the first note is played. While the guitarist is noodling aimlessly and the singer is arguing with himself about whether that scarf is too much, you're already in pre-show survival mode. You've built a one-man orchestra - every piece wired with potential betrayal. Before soundcheck even starts, you're already knee deep in troubleshooting. The laptop boots up. The MIDI controller connects. Your main synth loads the right patch - except it doesn't. You scroll through menus, trying not to panic. The secondary synth is too quiet. Something's glitching. You reroute cables. Check your mixer. Pray to whatever cosmic entity governs MIDI stability. Meanwhile, your bandmates are at the bar, blissfully unaware that you're in the middle of a silent, high-stakes tech crisis. To them, you look calm, composed, in control. They have no idea you're mentally defusing a bomb. And that's just soundcheck.

Once the set starts, you're not just playing. You're piloting a spaceship. Left hand locked on the bassline because the bassist *'wants to leave more space.'* Right hand juggling chords, melodies, or adding some atmospheric swell that makes the song sound five times bigger than it actually is. One foot's locked on the sustain pedal, the other's toggling through effects or triggering samples. Your brain's running four different checklists - listening for cues, anticipating disasters, and adjusting settings in real time.

The guitarist is lost in another self-indulgent solo. The singer is busy making eye contact with someone in the crowd. The drummer is still hopefully on tempo. Then it happens - the nightmare moment. Something always goes sideways. A note hangs too long. A pad doesn't trigger. Suddenly, your entire rig goes silent. And for a few horrifying

seconds, it's just you and the void. Your brain instantly enters crisis mode. Is it a cable? Power issue? Did the DAW freeze? Did the laptop crash? You check connections, unplug, replug, reboot - mash buttons like you're trying to reset the Matrix. You glance at the sound guy. He looks at you with a face that says,
"This is your problem, man."
Your bandmates? Oblivious. The guitarist extends his solo for the third time. The singer struts harder. If he notices at all, the drummer fills every available space with unnecessary drum rolls. By the time you fix it, the moment is gone. The damage is done. After the set, when you try to explain what happened?
"Oh. Didn't notice anything."

You're the shadow that gives their sound its shape. You bring depth, atmosphere, and cinematic texture. You make them feel bigger than they actually are. And yet, if you do your job perfectly... they don't even know you're there.

The One Alliance That Matters

You have one ally. One person who understands your struggle. Not the bassist, who's always in his own groove, no matter the situation. Definitely not the guitarist, who sees you as a minor inconvenience in his quest for sonic dominance. Not the singer, whose primary concern is whether the reverb on his mic makes him sound 'ethereal.' And not the drummer, who's still mad his toms got muted during soundcheck.

No, the only person who gets it - the only one who truly sees you - is the sound guy. He's not technically in the band, but he's close enough to see what you're dealing with better than anyone else. You don't have to speak much. In fact, you rarely do. But there's an unspoken bond between keyboardists and sound guys, forged in the quiet, painful knowledge that without them, the band would sound like a train wreck on fire. The guitarist is throwing a tantrum about his tone? The sound guy meets your eyes across the stage. No words are needed. You both understand. The singer is demanding "more me" for the seventh time tonight. A shared sigh, a subtle shake of the head, and a silent understanding: We're all dealing with a lot here.

He respects your gear. He never rolls his eyes at your synth rig or questions why you need so many buttons. If anything, he leans in, intrigued, and asks what you're running. More importantly? He actually listens to your mix. While the rest of the band fights for dominance, he's the only one who notices when your pad disappears from the verse or your synth lead gets swallowed by the guitar wall. He keeps your sound alive in a way the audience will never realize, because if he's doing his job right, they'll never even notice. And for that, he has earned your eternal gratitude.

Your conversations with him aren't loud, dramatic, or full of self-importance. They're technical, efficient, and completely free of ego. While the guitarist complains about "losing his tone" and the drummer insists his snare needs more punch, you and the sound guy are having a real conversation. To everyone else, it sounds like some alien dialect - half tech jargon, half telepathy - but you both speak it fluently.

"You think I should cut some of the low mids on this patch? Feels a little bloated."

He barely glances up from the board, already shooting from the hip.

"Yeah, a small dip around 250Hz should clean it up."

You make the adjustment, play a few notes, and nod in approval. He listens for a second, then leans in slightly.

"Man, that reverb profile is sick. What are you running?"

"Lexicon PCM," you reply, keeping it casual. "Dialed back so it doesn't drown the vocals."

He smirks - appreciative, respectful. You don't need to explain why. He already knows. You both do. No further words are necessary. This is a sacred alliance, built not on ego but on a shared understanding that the rest of the band is a lost cause without the two of you.

Of course, even he has limits. For all his power at the mixing desk, even the sound guy can't perform miracles. He can't stop the guitarist from cranking his amp past the point of distortion hell. He can't convince the singer that a delay effect won't fix his pitch issues. He can't stop the bassist from claiming he 'can't hear anything,' even when he's just lost in his own world. But he can do one thing. He can keep you in the mix. He can make sure that when you play that crucial pad, that swelling synth, that deep, resonant chord - you don't just exist. You are heard. In this world of live music, that nod from him is all the recognition you'll ever need.

Between the Notes

Most of the time, you're a phantom presence in the band. Heard but unnoticed. If you disappeared mid-set, it would probably take two full songs before anyone realized. Yet, every so often, when the universe aligns just right, someone recognizes your existence. It's never for long, but when it happens, you savor it.

One night, the PA dies mid-show. The crowd whispers, and the singer's poised breath turns into silence. The monitors are dead, and only the nervous shuffle of musicians fills the air. The guitarist plucks at his strings, the bassist stares into space, and the drummer, unfazed, keeps hitting random things. The sound guy is nowhere in sight... Then, all eyes turn to you. Because if anyone can fix this, it's you.

You set your drink down, wade through the mess of cables, and make a quick fix at the mixer. A flick of a switch, and the sound returns. The guitarist claps you on the back, and the singer whispers, "Thanks, man."

For that one glorious moment, you're the hero.

It happens again - but this time, it's subtler. The band decides to "strip it back and go raw" for a song, claiming they don't need your 'extra layers.' You keep your hands off the keys. No one says anything, but your channel is silent. They launch into the set, assuming it'll be fine. But something's off. The transitions feel thin. The air, once full, is now hollow. The guitarist cranks his delay pedal, the bassist plays louder, and the drummer fills in - none of it works. Then someone mutters, "Where's the keys?"

You've made your presence known, even in absence. They may not say thanks, but you can feel the relief as you sit at the keyboard and press a single chord. The song breathes again.

In these rare moments, they acknowledge the missing pieces. You play your quiet, essential role - without the glory. No one will say, *'Wow, the keys made that track.'*

But they know. And you know they know.

The sound guy walks by after the show, tired and unassuming, and says quietly,

"Man, your sound was on point tonight."

You really don't need further praise. His acknowledgment, though very brief, is worth more than a standing ovation.

Chapter 5

Center of the Universe

A Legend in His Own Mind

"To command a voice is to shape the air itself. It's not just sound. It is a declaration. A demand for attention no one can dismiss.

Where others fade into the mix, you rise above it. You stand where you can't be ignored - each note a battle cry, every breath bending the will of those who listen."

- The Eternal Spotlight of an Ever-Fading Star

The Day You Found the Mic - And the Mirror

You didn't just discover the microphone. You found your destiny - and an unshakable belief that the world needed to hear you.

It started with a hairbrush, a half-broken boombox, and a living room that became an arena. You didn't just sing. You performed... The couch was your stage, and the mirror? Your first audience. Every note, every exaggerated pose, every dramatic facial expression wasn't about sound. It was about presence.

Your first 'real' gig wasn't exactly a big break. A school talent show, most of the audience was made up of disinterested parents forced to attend. But to you, it was career-defining. You spent days choosing the perfect outfit. Your dad's oversized blazer seemed rockstar enough - hyping yourself up for the performance of a lifetime and rehearsing in the mirror until your reflection staged its own walkout.
The performance itself was a fever dream of voice cracks, missed lines, and one overly ambitious spin move that nearly sent you off the stage. The crowd winced. A teacher gasped. Somewhere in the background, a janitor started sweeping like the show had already ended. And then - applause. Genuine or polite, it didn't matter. You had tasted the high. That was the moment it all clicked. The notes, the chords, the technique - those were fine. But what really mattered was being seen. Standing in the center of it all. The one they clapped for.

Your first actual gig wasn't a stadium, but it felt like one.
A grimy dive bar called The Rusty Nail, where the walls leaked sound and possibly mold. The "stage" was a warped piece of plywood that creaked every time you moved. One mic stand leaned like it had given up on life, and the

monitors buzzed with the low hum of electrical regret. The place reeked of spilt beer and ancient ashtrays - even though smoking indoors had been banned for years.

The crowd maxed out at twelve. Half were your friends. The rest were regulars - seasoned drinkers who didn't appreciate having their darts game interrupted. One of them argued with a jukebox that wasn't even plugged in... Another spent your entire set shouting requests for songs that didn't exist.

You stepped onstage, mic trembling in your hand, convinced this would be the night someone "discovered" you. You had moves. You had banter. You wore a jacket heavy enough to qualify as stage equipment.

The set was a disaster. Jumbled verses. Awkward pauses and silence. A barfly yelled,
"Turn down the vocals!"
The mic smelled like beer and humiliation. You tried a dramatic move that left you disoriented and facing the wrong direction. But then - five glorious seconds. One note. Nailed.
Someone from the back shouted,
"You rock, dude!"
And that was all you needed. You were hooked. You weren't just that kid in a blazer anymore. You were a frontman in training. You hadn't earned the spotlight yet. But now, you knew where it lived.

From that day forward, you knew: You weren't meant to blend in. You were born to be a star.

Just Here for the Spotlight

The moment you picked up a microphone, you knew - this was it. The ultimate advantage. The rockstar effect. That primal, universal truth: singers are irresistible.

You had it all planned out.

The set ends, the lights hit just right, and you're still glowing with onstage electricity. You lean against the bar - cool, effortless, drenched in just enough sweat to look passionate but not deranged. And then, they arrive. The ones who felt something. A lip bite, a lingering gaze, maybe a whispered confession about how that song changed them. A number on a napkin. An invitation for a private encore. Maybe - just maybe - you'd unlocked the true power of being a musician.

Then reality kicks in. Your first post-show interaction? Some guy asking if you do weddings. Or a middle-aged couple gushing over "that one song" - the one you didn't even write the lyrics for. That intense eye contact from the front row? Not adoration. Just someone trying to get the bartender's attention.

Fine. One off night. The next show will be different. It isn't. As it turns out, being a lead singer isn't a dating cheat code - it's an unpredictable gamble. Sure, sometimes the rockstar effect works. But most of the time, you finish the set looking less like a mysterious artist and more like someone who lost a fight with a lawn sprinkler. The shirt's ruined. Hair plastered to your face. Voice, shot. Whatever mystique you had at the start of the night has been obliterated by sweat, exhaustion, and bad lighting. And even if someone is interested, they quickly realize they're not dating a person. They're dating a concept. No matter how the conversation starts, it always circles back to you. Your process. Your lyrics. The deep artistic vision behind your latest song - which, let's be honest, is also about you.

Then comes the most humbling reality check: people assume you're onstage for attention, not because you have a tortured soul. No matter how heartfelt your lyrics are or how much emotion you pour into them, the audience is 99% sure you love the sound of your own voice. Which, in fact, isn't entirely wrong.

But you refuse to give up. Because sometimes, it actually works. There are nights when everything clicks - the crowd hangs on your every word, someone is making intense eye contact, and you know a post-show conversation is about to go somewhere good.

So, you try again. You saunter up to the bar, still drenched in post-performance glory, convinced you're radiating pure rockstar magnetism - when, in reality, you smell like broken dreams and a van with no air-conditioning. But you commit. You lean in, drop your voice just enough to make it count, and go for something smooth.

"So, what was your favorite song tonight?"

A harmless, confident lead-in.

She hesitates. Then delivers the soul-crushing reply:

"Oh... Uuuh... the cover!"

The cover... The one song you didn't sing - the one the guitarist hijacked while you were taking a sip of water.

You shake it off. Maybe she's nervous. Perhaps she needs a little charm. You try again - direct, undeniable. You mention the ballad. That one. The one you saw her reacting to. The one that was practically written for this exact scenario. She laughs politely, the kind of laugh that carries absolutely zero sincerity.

"Wait, what? Sorry, I wasn't listening."

You inhale sharply. It's fine. You've been here before. You pivot, change the approach, make it personal. You tell her you wrote that song about someone like her. It's vague enough to feel intimate, to let her fill in the blanks with whatever romantic fantasy she prefers. For a second, it seems to land. She tilts her head, considering, then shrugs with a half-hearted "Aww... That's so sweet!"

It's not an answer. It's an exit strategy. And before you can salvage it, she's already turning toward her friend.

It's fine. There's still time. You try again - the casual invitation, the golden ticket - the next gig. She smiles, nods, and gives the kind of overly enthusiastic "Yeah, maybe..." people say when they have zero intention of following through.

You could stop here. You probably should. Instead, you push your luck. You lean in and deliver the line that should've sealed it from the start:

"You don't have to go home alone tonight."

She barely hesitates before delivering the final, crushing blow.

"Oh... I'm here with my boyfriend."

The words settle just long enough for you to realize your fatal mistake. The boyfriend - the one you somehow failed to notice, despite him standing next to her the entire time - turns toward you. There is no tension. No fight. Just a silent moment of mutual understanding. He winks. You nod.

And just like that, you're gone. Back to the bar. Back to reassessing your entire life. At least until the next gig. Because there will be a next one. There usually is. And deep down, we both know - you'll keep trying.

Eternal Rivalries:

You vs. The Band

Being the singer isn't just about delivering lyrics - it's about survival. You're not just fighting stage fright or mic feedback. You're fighting them - your so-called bandmates who seem to think they're just as important as you. They say it's about the music. They call you overdramatic. But in reality, they're just obstacles. And whether they admit it or not, every one of them is gunning for your spotlight.

The guitarist is the worst. You could graciously introduce him to the crowd - give him his little solo moment - but it's never enough. He plays like the entire band is his personal backing track. He'll shred through rehearsal like you're not even there. Then he spends the next hour walking you through chord voicings you never asked for. He talks in "tones" and "feels" and pretends he doesn't care about attention - until someone compliments his solo.

"Dude, that melted faces."

And you'll have to stand there, pretending it doesn't kill you that this glorified background musician got the one compliment you wanted. But of course, you smile. You let him have it because someone has to be the bigger person.

Then there's the drummer. You respect him. You really do. He keeps the band together. But he doesn't get it. To him, music should be rigid, predictable, always 'locked in.' But that's not how emotion works. You know a song needs space to breathe. A lingering pause before the next lyric. A perfectly stretched-out phrase, hanging just enough to make the crowd ache for the resolution. And what does he do? He bulldozes it. Every time. You've finally built the perfect dramatic silence - BAM. He crashes in like a drunk airline pilot skidding onto the wrong runway.

The worst part is he doesn't even realize what he's doing. In his head, he's the foundation. The timekeeper. The backbone. The guy who thinks he's holding it all together. But if you decide to stretch a note, to hold a moment, to let the weight of a song settle into the crowd - does he follow? No. He resists. So you push. You test him. You hold it longer. And just when you think, maybe - just maybe - he'll let the tension hang... CRASH. Right back in like an overeager substitute teacher desperate to keep the class on schedule.

The bassist doesn't argue. He doesn't roll his eyes like the guitarist or sabotage you like the drummer. He just watches. Silently. Judgmentally. Every offbeat vocal run, every dramatic pause, every impulsive tempo shift - he clocks it all. And yet, no matter what you do, he never says a word. Just subtly adjusts - an unspoken apology to the universe for your existence. And that's almost worse. The guitarist is arrogant. The drummer pushes back. But the bassist exists in a quiet little bubble of unwavering competence, doing his job like he's in the middle of an earthquake drill. If you set fire to the setlist mid-song, he'd barely blink. No panic. No frustration. Just a shift in his playing, a minor adjustment to keep the song from collapsing. It's infuriating. How is he so calm all the time? So unbothered - never cracks, never loses it, never complains. You know you drive him insane. You have to. Still, he plays on - grounded, unfazed, proving with every note that if anyone in this band can survive without you... it's him.

The keys guy is technically on your side - he never fights you directly. But somehow, his empire keeps expanding. One day, it was one keyboard. Then two. Then a laptop. Then a pedalboard. Then enough cables to wire a surveillance van. He never says he's taking more space. He just does. And if you get too close, he gives you that look, the one that says,

'Touch one cable and you'll meet your maker.'

You could confront him, but honestly? You need him.

He makes everything sound bigger - until he doesn't. Because if he wants to, he can shift the entire mood of a song. Too much reverb? You're a lounge singer at an airport bar. One cheesy synth pad? Now your heartbreaking ballad sounds like a rejected soap opera theme. And worst of all is that he knows exactly what he's doing. He waits for that moment when you get a little too theatrical to slip in a sound that makes your sincerity feel like a parody.

But of all your rivals, the sound guy is the puppet master. He doesn't just work the mix - he controls it. You don't ask for much. A little more vocal in the monitor. A touch of reverb. Just enough presence to cut through the wall of guitars. And yet, every time, it's a gamble. One set, your mic is barely audible. The next, it's dry enough to peel paint. And just when you think you finally have the balance right, he cranks the delay and turns your voice into an echo chamber of shame. Worst of all, you can't call him out. Not really. Because if you do? Your mic might just "accidentally" cut out during your big mid-set speech.

At the end of the night, the guitarist believes his solos are the reason people showed up. The drummer thinks you have no timing. The bassist silently judges your every move. The keyboardist low-key hopes you trip over his pedalboard. And the sound guy would mute you if he could. They won't admit it. But without them, you're just a guy with a mic. And without you, they're just some dudes playing background music. They can resent you all they want. But the truth is, people came for you. And no matter how hard they fight it - they know it.

The Struggle for Stage Space

The moment you step into the lights, mic in hand, you can feel it - this is your stage. Or at least, it should be. The energy shifts. The crowd is with you. The moment is yours... until someone else decides it isn't.

The guitarist inches closer like a territorial dog marking new ground. The drummer, allergic to subtlety, picks the worst possible moment to throw in a dramatic fill that shatters whatever atmosphere you were building. The bassist lurks in the shadows, tracking every exaggerated gesture like he's taking notes for a future intervention. And the keyboardist expands his setup like an invasive species - one synth at a time - until half the stage is a mess of glowing buttons and cables. It's not an argument - it's a cold war of movement. A tactical dance of elbows and egos waged in inches. You step forward. So do they. You find the light. They shift into it. No one says a word, but everyone knows what's happening.

As expected, he's at the front again - hair flinging, foot on the monitor, pretending he's closing out a festival. You let him have it for now... But you're already plotting your counter-move. The only problem? This isn't his song. It isn't even his moment. So you time your counterattack. As his solo builds, you step forward - right into his space. Casual. Effortless. A mic stand lean. Or just enough shoulder to make him adjust. He doesn't even realize he's been edged out until the lights shift and the eyes come back to you.
Mission accomplished...

Then it's the drummer. Your eyes lock. The song is hanging on a breath, the crowd leaning in. You stretch the silence just long enough to make them ache for what comes next. And then - BOOM. A snare roll. A hi-hat splash.

A cymbal crash that no one asked for. The moment shatters. You don't turn around. You don't need to. He's already grinning, soaked and breathless, thrilled to have made the quiet part loud again. But you wait. The song drops back into its final chorus, soft and slow. The band follows your lead. And then, when it counts, you reclaim it. You stretch the final note, steal the stillness, and soak in the attention. The drummer holds back. He knows better than to ruin the ending - this time.

The bassist never moves. Never fights. But he watches everything - every mic-stand pose, every hair flip, every impulsive tempo shift you spring mid-set. He never says a word, but you can feel his disapproval like an aura. You break the rhythm, he patches it up. You add drama, and he quietly stabilizes it. But one day, he'll let you fall. And when he does, it's because you deserved it.

And the keys guy? His silent expansion continues. You step back - just one step - and suddenly, you're tangled in his empire. Cables. Pedals. Gear with buttons you've never seen. He says it's for "atmosphere." You say it's a silent coup. But the truth is that he's winning. And worse - you need him to.

By the end of the set, nothing has changed. The guitarist is still overstepping. The drummer is still overplaying. The bassist is still holding the band together in stoic silence. And the keyboardist is now occupying almost half of the stage. But you're still in the center. You're the one they came to see. The lights find you first. The eyes follow your every move. And no matter how many inches they steal - no matter how many moments they try to hijack - when the night ends, you're still the show. And if they ever forget... You'll make damn sure they remember.

The Wardrobe Saga:

Dressing Like You Mean It

You've always known that what you wear on stage is just as important as what you sing. Your bandmates will throw on whatever doesn't smell like a dumpster. But you? You get it. The right outfit isn't just style - it's strategy.

Your pre-show ritual doesn't start with vocal warmups or setlist discussions - it begins in front of your closet, staring down the most critical decision of the night. The outfit. It's not just about looking good - it sets the tone, creates the atmosphere, and locks you into the persona. Are you going for mysterious and moody or electric and unhinged? Do you need leather? Sequins? Layers? The wrong choice could derail your entire performance.

While the band is at the venue, setting up their gear like responsible musicians, you're engaged in a far more important battle. Fifteen minutes later, you're down to two scarves so identical you start questioning reality itself. This is the real struggle.

Every legendary frontman has a signature piece. Something that makes it clear they're not just in the band. They are the band. For some, it's a jacket so heavy it turns every set into a full-body endurance test. For others, it's a scarf collection so extensive it could double as stage decoration. Maybe it's a hat so oversized, your entire set becomes a guessing game - is it fashion, or performance anxiety with a brim? Your bandmates will mock you for being extra, but they know they could never pull it off.

Functionality? That's for session musicians.

Comfort? That's for roadies.

You're here to make an impact. If your outfit lets you breathe properly, move freely, or get through a set without constant readjustment - you've already lost.

You accept the trade-offs. Your pants are too tight for anything beyond careful pacing. Your boots weren't made for escape, but then again, when has that ever been an option? Your shirt is purely decorative, and removing your jacket mid-set is a tactical operation. One wrong move and the show's over.

But none of that matters. Because at the end of the night, as the last chord fades and the crowd shuffles toward the bar, someone will find you. They'll push past the other band members - past the guitarist who played an entire solo behind his head, past the drummer who nearly collapsed from exhaustion - just to get to you. And every time, without fail, they'll say,

"Dude, your outfit is incredible."

Not "great vocals." Not "amazing stage presence." Not even "tight set." It's just validation of the only thing that really matters. And that's how you know you made the right choice.

The Mic Is Your Sword, and the Stage Is Your Battlefield

The mic isn't just equipment - it's the key to your entire existence. It's the difference between being ignored and being unforgettable. You don't just hold it. You wield it. And the stage isn't just a platform - it's a battlefield. Not against some imaginary enemy, but against obscurity, mediocrity, and occasionally, your own bandmates.

Soundcheck is supposed to be a technical process - a few "check-one-twos" and some quick level tweaks before the doors open. But to you, it's an opportunity. A preview. A mini-concert, whether the band likes it or not.

The sound guy expects a mic test. You give him a performance. First, a whispered phrase to test the lows. Then a mid-range warm-up - casual, intimate, maybe a bit too rehearsed. And finally, the full send: a high-drama vocal run. Eyes closed. One hand to the chest. Head tilted just enough to imply profound personal anguish. One breath away from collapse... By the time you finish, the sound guy has stopped pretending to adjust anything. The guitarist is on his phone. The bassist's at the bar. The drummer, furious, starts hitting cymbals at random just to shut you up. Soundcheck is over. You win.

Once the show starts, the war begins. Your arsenal of signature moves - crafted through years of instinct, ego, and pure theatrical necessity - is in full effect. *'The Air Grab,'* a desperate reach into the void, clutching at nothing and yet everything. *'The Mic Stand Lean'* - a delicate balance between effortless cool and a potential wipeout. *'The Point'* - sharp, deliberate, a move that makes every person in the crowd think,

'Yeah, this song is about me.'

And finally, *'The Slow Turn'* - a mid-verse pivot with the

perfect pacing - slow enough to seem deliberate, fast enough to avoid looking like you forgot where you were going. Separately, they are powerful. Together? They are a performance.

But for all your mastery, you have one mortal enemy: the mic cable. It is chaos incarnate. No matter how much you prepare, it finds a way to betray you, wrapping around your feet, knotting itself mid-song, and threatening your dignity with every step. At best, you untangle yourself smoothly, making it part of the act. Worst case? You trip, stumble, recover - then immediately blame the guitarist. Because obviously, it was his fault.

By the last song, you're drenched. Exhausted. Standing in the wreckage of whatever just happened. The band rolls their eyes. But they know. Without you, it's not a show. Without your theatrics, it's just music. And who wants that?

The Eternal War with the Sound Guy

It's an unspoken rivalry, but both sides know it exists. You and the sound guy have been at odds since your first gig. Maybe it started when he "forgot" to turn your mic on at the beginning of the set. Or it was the way he exhaled a little too loudly when you asked for more reverb. Or maybe it's the simple fact that, no matter what you request, your vocals never sound quite right. This isn't just a disagreement. It's a full-blown war, and neither side is surrendering.

It always begins the same way. The band kicks in, and the energy builds, but something feels wrong. You can't hear yourself properly. Your voice is drowning beneath the instruments, swallowed whole by the sonic chaos. You glance at the booth and signal for more vocals. A small adjustment. You nod. Still not enough.

"A little more."

Another tweak. Now, the bass is overwhelming everything.

"Can we take some bass out? It's muddying my tone."

The mix shifts again. Better, but now it's too clean. Too sterile. Something feels off.

"Okay, let's warm it up. A little more presence. But not too much. Just a bit brighter. But still deep. You know what I mean?"

At this point, the sound guy is staring at the wall, wondering if he should have gone to trade school instead. The guitarist has stopped pretending to tune. The drummer is tapping his sticks against his knees. The bassist leans against his amp, absently adjusting his strap, his expression somewhere between boredom and quiet resignation - already halfway to the bar in his mind. The audience - completely unaware - just wants you to get on with it. You give one last nod, satisfied. For now. But the moment the next song starts, you already know - it's still not quite right.

You've been burned too many times to trust the reverb settings. Some nights, it's nonexistent, leaving your voice painfully dry, exposed in a way that makes even the best vocal runs sound like a public speaking nightmare. Other nights, he drowns your voice in so much echo that you sound less like a singer and more like a lost soul calling for help from the bottom of a well. You step back and lock eyes with him across the venue. He stares back, blank, unbothered. This was intentional. He knows you know. And he does not care. Because you should have known better than to ask for "just the right amount." In his world, that amount does not exist.

And then, of course, comes the muted mic conspiracy. It always happens at the worst possible moment. The song ends, the energy is perfect, and the crowd is locked in. It's time for your big moment - a heartfelt speech, something deep, something raw, something they'll actually feel.

You step forward, grip the mic, take a breath - silence. Nothing. You tap the mic - still nothing. The sound guy shrugs.

"Technical issues..."

Sure. Convenient. Especially since the guitarist's amp has never once cut out mid-solo. The audience watches as you fumble for an alternative. The drummer's mic is the closest, but it's set for someone sitting down, leaving you hunched over awkwardly, delivering your speech at knee level. The moment is gone. Coincidence? Maybe. But you have your doubts. Of course, if you asked him, he'd tell a different story. From his perspective, you are the problem. You are the reason soundcheck takes three times longer than necessary. You are the reason the guitarist keeps turning up. You are why the bassist mumbles,

"Just play through it..."

He braces himself the moment you hit the stage. He knows you'll start adjusting your in-ear monitors thirty seconds into the first song. He knows you'll wave at him mid-set with some vague hand signal that means absolutely nothing. He knows that no matter what he does, you will never be completely happy with the mix. From your perspective, he's doing this on purpose. From his? He's just trying to survive you.

So maybe he did turn your mic down a little more than necessary. Perhaps it was an accident. Or maybe it wasn't. But just think about it - if you were him, wouldn't you?

Disasterclass: When the Spotlight Betrays You

Of course, not every disaster is someone else's fault. Sometimes, the spotlight turns on you - and there's no one left to blame. Being a singer comes with risk. Unlike the rest of the band, you can't just stand in one place, staring at an instrument. You are the show. You have to move, command attention, and bring the energy. When it all clicks, the audience is in sync, and the lights hit just right, your performance creates something greater than the sum of its parts - pure magic. But when it spirals out? Catastrophic. And worse, burned into your memory forever. Every frontman has those moments - the humiliations, the failed theatrics, the brutal reality checks. The ones that keep you up at night, staring at the ceiling, whispering,
"Why?"
Maybe it was a mic failure. A mistimed stage move. A crowd engagement attempt that backfired hard. And yet, no matter how many times you crash and burn, you somehow keep making the same mistakes.

It always starts with confidence. The lights. The energy. That hum of anticipation in your chest. You step forward, grip the mic, take a deep breath. Dead air. Silence. Not sabotage, just a perfect storm of bad timing and betrayal by the gods of live sound. You glance at the booth. The sound guy shrugs, already pretending this has nothing to do with him. The guitarist starts noodling to cover the awkwardness. The drummer, sensing panic, throws in a cymbal roll - because if there's chaos, he's contributing. The bassist doesn't even look up. He's seen this too many times. Eventually, the mic cracks to life. But the moment's already lost. The audience is mildly amused. You, on the other hand, are left wondering if the sound guy "forgot" to unmute you...

or if this was just another round in your eternal war.

And then there's the lyrics blackout - every singer's worst fear. You've sung this song a hundred times. You wrote it. You know every note, every phrasing, every shift in dynamics. And yet, mid-verse, your brain betrays you. Blank. Empty. Gone. For a second, you consider faking it - mumble through, throw in a vague syllable. But panic takes over, and suddenly, you're just making up nonsense.

"Looooove... in the raaaain, we are... the... uh... feeeelings?"

Nailed it.

The guitarist shoots you a sideways glance, hovering between amusement and disappointment. The bassist, who definitely knows the lyrics, raises an eyebrow. The drummer is already laughing. There's no saving it now. The only option is to commit - step back dramatically, hold a long, emotional note, and pray the crowd is drunk enough to fill in the blanks.

And if forgetting the words isn't bad enough, the failed rockstar move is always waiting to humble you. Somewhere in your mind, you believe you're as effortlessly cool as every legendary frontman before you. And sometimes, bad judgment and adrenaline convince you to prove it. Maybe it's a mic stand twirl, meant to look effortlessly smooth - except the mic stand flies out of your hands, crashes into the drummer's kit, and nearly takes out a cymbal. Maybe it's the high kick - meant to be dramatic and powerful - but instead, your foot meets the bassist's pedalboard with a sickening thud. His signal dies instantly. The song collapses. And you're frozen in place, processing the exact moment you became the villain of the set.

And then there's the knee drop - the most dangerous move in your arsenal. In theory, it's pure emotion. In reality? It's agony. Your knees hit the stage like you just jumped off a roof onto concrete. The rest of the set is spent limping, wondering how it didn't hurt at all when you rehearsed it on the motel carpet two hours ago. No one checks if you're okay. The band's too busy laughing.

Of course, if physical injury doesn't get you, the overhyped crowd moment will. Nothing is worse than trying to get the audience involved and failing miserably. You throw your arms up, signaling for a clap-along. A couple of weak, off-time claps come from the back. That's it. You try again, louder, more enthusiasm this time. Still nothing.

"Everybody sing it with me!"

You yell, thrusting the mic toward the crowd, waiting for that euphoric explosion of voices screaming the lyrics back at you.

Silence.

You glance at the band for backup, but suddenly, they're all painfully preoccupied. The guitarist is staring at his fretboard like he just discovered a secret chord that will change music forever. The bassist, arms crossed, is watching the guitarist watch his fretboard, nodding thoughtfully as if he, too, is on the verge of enlightenment. The drummer, twirling a stick between his fingers, watches the bassist watch the guitarist, barely suppressing a grin. The keyboardist is suddenly very busy adjusting a knob that does absolutely nothing. And the sound guy just watches, shaking his head like a man who's lost all faith in humanity.

They all act like they didn't see what just happened. Like they don't even know you. Not one of them will help. And that's something you just have to live with. You lower the mic, pass it off as a crowd energy test, and die a little inside.

And if that wasn't bad enough, there's the premature exit. The set is reaching its massive, epic finale. You hit the last note, throw your arms out triumphantly, and stride confidently off stage. Except... the band is still playing. You misread the ending. You thought that was the moment, but the guitarist is still mid-solo. You stop dead in your tracks.

The crowd sees. The band sees. The guitarist, lost in artistic ecstasy, does not.You could walk back out and pretend nothing happened, but now it's weird. So you just stand there, frozen, looking less like a rockstar and more like someone who got lost on the way to the bathroom. The only thing worse than leaving too early? Coming back mid-solo, forcing you to hover awkwardly, pretending it was all part of the plan. No escape. No dignity. Just discomfort. Pure and uncut. You didn't mean to end the show early. But you did. And now everyone knows.

The Show Must Go Wrong

(Stumble, Laugh, Repeat)

No matter how much experience you have, no matter how many shows you've played, no matter how much you've convinced yourself that you are untouchable - you will embarrass yourself onstage. It's inevitable. The moments you'd kill to forget will haunt you forever. And the worst part is that the band will never let you live them down.

The guitarist brings it up at every rehearsal - usually right before launching into a ten-minute solo. The bassist won't even say anything - he'll smirk at the exact wrong time, letting you know that, yes, he still remembers. The drummer re-enacts it purely for sport, complete with exaggerated gestures and sound effects. And the keyboardist will probably add a comedic synth sting the next time you try something dramatic to remind you who really runs the show. But the audience? They won't care about your mistakes. They won't remember the crash - or the blackout moment you're still cringing over. Just how you recovered. If you play it off like it never happened, if you sell it like it was intentional - then you win.

So you laugh. Shake it off. Let the band roast you, knowing full well that their turn is coming soon. And when you step back onstage for the next show, you do what every real frontman does: You act like it never happened. Because in rock music, it was never about perfection. It was always about the show.

One More Song!

For all the disasters, rivalries, and humiliations, there are nights when everything clicks. The crowd is in your hands, the sound is flawless, and for one moment, you are precisely the rockstar you always imagined. These nights keep you coming back. They make up for every missed lyric, and every botched crowd interaction.

The first sign that it's happening? You nail the note. Most of the time, you land somewhere in the general vicinity, close enough that nobody notices the micro-adjustments you're making to compensate. But not tonight. Tonight, you go for it. That note - the one that betrayed you in rehearsal, cracked in soundcheck, the one you nearly skipped - soars. For the first time, the guitarist looks impressed. The drummer yells something approving, hammering his snare in solidarity. Even the bassist - who treats enthusiasm like a disease - gives you a subtle nod. And the audience? They felt that one.

You hold onto the moment for just a second too long, letting the energy sink into your bones. It's euphoric, untouchable, pure rockstar electricity. And then, because the universe has a cruel sense of humor, you immediately miss your next entrance - too busy basking in your greatness.

But it doesn't matter. Tonight, the audience is with you. You can tell. You can feel it. And then, in the middle of the set, it happens... The moment every singer dreams about. You step back, mic outstretched, just to see if they'll sing the lyrics back to you. And they do. At first, it's hesitant. A few scattered voices, unsure. Then, it builds and grows. It gains momentum. Suddenly, it's everywhere - off-key, chaotic, perfect. For a split second, you do nothing. Just stand there, arms wide, letting it wash over you. And in that moment, the dream isn't just alive... it's real. It's overwhelming.

Your bandmates, unfortunately, do not share the moment. The guitarist throws you an exaggerated eye-roll, already preparing himself for the next six months of you bringing this up at every rehearsal. The drummer gives you a deeply patronizing “Aww, look at him.”

The bassist mutters,

“We’re never gonna hear the end of this...”

And they’re right. But none of it matters - because the crowd is still singing. Then, the impossible happens.

The song ends. You’re spent. Victorious. Ready to take your final bow, soak up the applause... and disappear into the night. And just as you take that first step toward the wings, you hear it. A single voice at first. Then another. Then a chorus, growing louder.

“One more song! One more song!”

You freeze, scanning the crowd in disbelief. Somehow, they’re still with you. Turning to your bandmates, wide-eyed, you act like it’s a miraculous surprise - not the exact scenario you’ve fantasized about every night of your life. The guitarist groans. The drummer shrugs. The bassist stares at the floor, calculating how many extra minutes this adds to his night. But you already know they’ll give in. Because no matter how much they claim to hate you, they hate looking ungrateful in front of a crowd even more. And so, one last song. One last moment. Because tonight? They wanted more.

These are the nights that keep you coming back. They make all the self-inflicted disasters, failed theatrics, and fights over stage space worth it. These nights are why you show up to another soundcheck. Why you put up with the guitarist’s ego, the drummer’s chaos, the bassist’s silent judgment, and the sound guy’s complete and utter disdain for your existence. Because for every ten trainwrecks, there’s one night where everything is perfect. And that’s enough to make you believe you were meant for this.

Never Look Back

Being a frontman isn't just about having a great voice - it's about owning the space, commanding attention, and making the audience believe in you. Some singers step on stage and immediately have it - the effortless presence, the magnetic pull, the ability to bend a room's energy with a glance.
You are not one of them.
But presence can be built. Command can be learned. And if you're willing to do what it takes, you won't just be some guy with a microphone. You'll be the show.

The transformation starts the first time you see yourself on video. You thought you were moving with intensity. What do you actually see? Stiff. Awkward. Hesitant. Instead of owning the stage, you look like you just wandered onto it by accident. It's a wake-up call. But you don't panic. You adjust. You plant your feet, move with purpose, and watch yourself in the mirror - not with vanity, but with brutal self-awareness. You refine how you hold the mic and take up space instead of shrinking into it. Somewhere in that process, something shifts.

At first, the mic stand feels like a liability - a clunky piece of gear that never cooperates. You go for a cool lean and nearly tip it over. You try to pick it up smoothly and fumble like a failed magic trick. You learn fast: the mic stand isn't just there for support - it's a weapon, a prop, an extension of you. Eventually, it stops feeling like an object and starts feeling like part of your hands. Or maybe something deeper, like it's wired into your entire existence.

How you arrive sets the tone before a single note is played. Legends don't shuffle onto the stage; they step into the spotlight like they were born there. You pick a song with a strong intro and practice repeatedly until the hesitation disappears. The first time you walk into a venue like you own it? People notice.

Mastering the crowd is the next test. The best frontmen don't just sing at an audience - they make them part of the show. It's not about throwing the mic out and hoping for a response. It's about building the moment, teasing it, leading them there so that when you finally step back and let them take over, they don't hesitate. The first time they scream the lyrics back, you almost forget to keep singing. And in that moment, you're not just performing. You're leading.

The hardest lesson is knowing when to stop moving. You start by assuming great frontmen are in constant motion. But then you watch the best of them - how they pause dramatically before a massive chorus, letting the audience hang in silence. You realize that stillness, when used at the right moment, can be louder than a scream.

Eventually, something deeper clicks. You stop playing the role and become it. You don't just rehearse. You don't just go through the motions. You walk into every room like you're stepping onto a stage. You talk like someone who expects to be listened to. You hold eye contact like you're delivering the most important line of your life. And when someone asks how you're doing, you don't say,

"Fine."

You don't say,

"Same as always."

You look them in the eye, and with absolute certainty, you say:

"Living the dream."

At first, it feels ridiculous. Then, one day, it doesn't.

Because great frontmen don't just play the part. They become it. And now - so have you. So grab the mic. Take the stage. And if it all derails completely, just pretend it was part of the act.

Chapter 6

The Gatekeeper of Chaos

The invisible force between you and total silence

"To shape sound is to wield power unseen. The band wails, the audience listens - but only you decide what they truly hear.

They curse you when it fails, yet never praise you when it sings. Such is the burden of the hidden architect."

- The Keeper of the Frequencies

How the Sound Guy Ended Up Controlling Everything

Every band has that one guy - the poor soul who, at some point, made the mistake of knowing too much. He didn't sign up for it. He fixed a buzzing cable once or, worse, correctly hooked up a DI box. Maybe he was the only one who understood gain staging. Or he actually read a manual. And from that moment, he was doomed. Now, every broken connection, faulty pedal, and mysteriously dead channel is his problem. He's not a professional. He doesn't have formal training. But because he's slightly less clueless than the rest of the band - which is a dangerously low bar - he has been anointed The Band's Tech Guy.

And then there's the other guy who knows exactly what he's doing. The one standing between the audience and a complete sonic disaster. The real audio engineer. Unlike the band's tech guy, he didn't accidentally stumble into this role. He trained for it. He studied it. He built a career around it. He's the one running sound at the venue, mixing in the studio, shaping how the audience hears a band. By now, nothing surprises him. He has worked with musicians who believe they are the first to request "more me" in the monitors. He's heard every excuse for bad playing. Every desperate attempt to blame the mix instead of the musician. "It sounded better at practice." Or "Can you add more punch to my bass?"

Even the delusional:

"My amp is special."

And, of course, the classic:

"Hey, can you turn me up?"

The answer to that last one is always no.

One is an unpaid hostage. The other - *theoretically* - a professional. But despite their differences, they share the same fate - musicians will always think they know more. And that's why the sound guy stopped arguing a long time ago. Instead, he plays the game. He smiles. He nods. He pretends to turn a knob that does nothing. He lets the guitarist believe his amp sounds perfect - when, in reality, he's been high-passing the low-end mud out of the mix the entire set. He allows the singer to bathe in reverb, knowing that by mid-show, he'll panic and ask if it's too much. The sound guy holds all the power. And when necessary, he uses it.

Soundcheck: Where Logic Goes to Die

For one brief, fragile moment, everything works. Levels are set, monitors dialed in, and the sound guy dares to believe - just this once - tonight might go smoothly. Then it begins.
"Hey, can I get more of me in the monitors?"
The guitarist starts the ritual.
A small tweak.
"Cool, thanks, man."
A minute later:
"Actually... just a bit more?"
Fine. Another bump. Another pause.
"A little more clarity? Can you make it punchier? I don't know, it just doesn't sound right."
And just like that, soundcheck collapses into a black hole of endless adjustments. The guitarist's requests inspire the singer. He now needs more reverb. Not for the venue. Not for the mix. For his soul.
"Just a touch more?"
The sound guy obliges, already predicting the future. By the third song, the singer will be drowning in his own cathedral of echoes, begging to be rescued from the canyon he built.

Then there's the bassist. Silent. Unnoticed. Until...
"I need more presence."
No one knows what that means - least of all the bassist. The sound guy pretends to tweak something. The bassist nods, satisfied.

And last but not least - the drummer. His role in soundcheck? Test the structural integrity of every microphone. The moment a mic is placed near his snare, he winds up like a medieval catapult and annihilates it with the force of an industrial accident. The entire venue winces as the sound guy scrambles to keep the channel from peaking into sheer devastation.

At this point, soundcheck isn't about sound anymore. It's a live psychological experiment in human stubbornness. The guitarist needs to believe his tone is perfect, so the sound guy fakes an adjustment, even though he's secretly cutting out the same muddy frequencies the guitarist keeps dialing in. The bassist's fader might as well be a placebo slider at this point. The singer is already lost inside his echo chamber.

By the time the doors open, the sound guy has accepted his fate. This isn't about achieving sonic perfection - it's about getting through the night without someone having an existential crisis over their mix.

Then comes the real sonic war. The guitarist starts off reasonable. He sets a sensible volume during soundcheck. The mix is balanced. Everything is peaceful. Then, midway through the first song, it begins. A tiny nudge of the volume knob. Nothing drastic. Just a touch of extra firepower. The sound guy exhales through his nose and compensates. A minute later - another adjustment. Louder. He looks up from the board, squinting at the stage. Did he just...? No. Maybe it's fine. Or it was his imagination. He takes a slow, measured breath and reminds himself to pick his battles. Another nudge. Now, it's undeniable. The mix is shifting. The guitar is creeping forward, devouring more sonic real estate with every passing verse. The sound guy debates whether to intervene, but he already knows how this story ends. By the third song, the war is over. It wasn't even close. The guitarist has seized control. His amp reigns supreme. The bassist is a whisper. The keys guy might as well be transmitting MIDI signals into outer space. The drummer, desperate to restore balance, has abandoned finesse entirely, hammering his kit with the force of a demolition crew, hoping sheer brutality will reclaim what the mix has stolen from him.

Lost in his own world, the guitarist doesn't notice the

audience wincing where they should be headbanging. He's beyond them now - beyond the band, beyond the music itself. He is speaking directly to the universe. The universe, however, is not responding. The sound guy checked out two songs ago. He's not even pretending to tweak things anymore. His only concern now is what he's ordering for dinner.

But before he lets the night slip away, he allows himself one small act of rebellion - a secret, invisible tweak to the mix. Just enough to spark a flicker of doubt. The guitarist squints at his amp and tilts his head. Something feels off. He looks out at the soundboard, searching for answers. The sound guy meets his gaze, expression blank.

"Everything's fine, man."

The guitarist hesitates, then reluctantly nods. The cycle continues. And then, the singer - drunk on self-importance - turns back to the board.

"Hey... is there too much reverb on my vocals?"

The sound guy exhales, reaches for a knob, turns it - without actually changing a thing.

"All set, man."

The singer nods, satisfied, oblivious to the fact that he is now performing inside an interdimensional ghost cave of his own creation. The sound guy leans back, arms crossed. He knows the game is over. He has won.

The Mix You Want vs. The Mix You Get

The studio was a world of precision. The strings shimmered, the snare cracked, and the bass rumbled deep in your chest. Every frequency was sculpted, and every note landed precisely as it should. This was how you were meant to sound.

Then came the live show. The first chord hit, and something felt off. Hollow mix. Thin guitars. Bass, gone. Drums somehow both too loud and barely there. Vocals, once sharp and soaring, lost in reverb. The sound wasn't broken - it was just unrecognizable. The precise, controlled mix you obsessed over in the studio had no place here. Out in the wild, sound had a mind of its own. Physics, bad wiring, and room acoustics waged war, twisting what once was perfect. The punch of the kick drum, gone. The warmth of the bass, either missing entirely or rattling the venue apart. Lost in the void, the guitarist kept turning up until he was all that remained. The singer, panicked, blamed the monitors, the sound guy, the room - anything but the truth settling in. This wasn't the sound of the record. It was something wilder, messier, and completely unpredictable. And maybe - just maybe - that was the whole point.

The sound guy had seen it all before. Every venue was a different battlefield, and every mix was doomed to collapse the second it left the safety of a controlled room. What worked in the studio meant nothing here. Boutique pedals, hand-wired amps, years of obsessive tone-chasing - none of it could fight the chaos of a live room. He could warn you that your perfect sound was slipping through your fingers. But it's better this way. Better to let you believe it can still be saved. Not because he's incompetent. Not because he's lazy. But because live sound doesn't work like that. And that's assuming the venue even has a sound system worth saving. Maybe the monitors cut out halfway through the set. Or the sound guy gave up an hour ago and is just riding out the storm.

The audience might love you. Your bandmates might have your back. But the final, deciding force between brilliance and disaster stands behind the mixing console. If the board is on your side, the mix feels effortless - tight guitars, pounding drums, vocals soaring over everything with clarity and power. If not, the chorus you poured your soul into sinks into mud. The solo you built an entire song around gets swallowed whole. That mic-drop moment you were banking on - gone. No pop, no signal, just the slow, creeping horror of a mic that inexplicably doesn't work. You will never know if it was an accident. Maybe the gear failed. Or maybe the venue's system was held together by duct tape and prayer. Perhaps it wasn't an accident at all.

Every audio engineer keeps a secret ranking system for bands. It's never talked about, never written down - but it exists. If you're in good standing, the mix is massive. Every instrument locked in, every note landing with power. But annoy the wrong person, and things unravel fast. Vocals buried, bass erased, a drum kit that feels like it's vanishing no matter how hard it's hit. Push it too far, and you start slipping into a world of "technical issues": a monitor dropout just before your big moment, a mysterious delay in the vocal mix, a fader dip right when the chorus hits. Could be bad luck. Could be a glitch. Could be... something else. Either way, you'll never be able to prove it. So respect the board. Respect the person behind it. Thank them. Maybe even buy them a drink. Because whether your band soars or sinks is never really up to you.

The Last Fader Drop

Every band thinks they can win over the sound guy. Some try technical jargon - *'Cut 500Hz to clean up the mud,'* or *'Give me some air at 10k'* - as if rattling off frequencies would earn special treatment.

Others launch into unsolicited breakdowns of their boutique pedalboard and hand-wired signal chain, convinced he'll care. He doesn't. He's heard it all.

Then there's the name-dropper.

"My last session was produced by [*insert famous producer name here*]."

Great. Is he here to save you? No. Then it's not the sound guy's problem.

Bribery works - but only if timed perfectly. Offer him a drink before the set, and he assumes you want something. Offer it after, once the cables are coiled and the chaos is over, and now you're speaking his language.

But none of it changes anything. The sound guy decides how your band sounds before you even strike the first chord. He has favorites - every engineer does. And while he'll still give everyone a balanced mix (he's a professional, after all), one member always gets a little extra love. And it's usually the keys guy. Why? Because he speaks fluent signal chain. He understands what "cut 500Hz" actually means. He doesn't blow up gear or scream for more reverb mid-song. His synths shimmer, his pads fill the room, and he's always the last one standing when the mix collapses.

Meanwhile, if you've been difficult all night, your fate is sealed - and you'll never be able to prove it. A tiny delay in the vocal mix. A monitor mute that lasts just long enough to rattle your confidence. A subtle feedback squeal that only happens during your solo. You adjust settings, chasing ghosts, while the sound guy watches - expressionless, unmoved, maybe even slightly amused. You'll walk off unsettled - something felt off, but you can't prove a thing. A flicker of feedback here, a missing vocal line there. Sabotage? A glitch? It could've been the venue. Or maybe you did something small and stupid that landed you in the sound guy's bad books.

The band starts packing. The singer's still onstage, soaking up compliments like a dying houseplant. The guitarist is mid-monologue about his gear to someone who stopped listening five minutes ago. The drummer has vanished - likely already two drinks deep. The bassist is loitering, waiting for acknowledgment that will never come.

And the sound guy is still there. Coiling cables. Erasing all evidence that your band ever happened. He doesn't need applause. Doesn't need thanks. Because when it's all over, he had the last word. He decided who soared, sank, and walked offstage, wondering what went wrong. Maybe it was bad luck. Perhaps it was just a glitch. Or you should've shaken his hand. Because at the end of the night, the sound guy holds all the power. And if you're lucky, he'll pretend he doesn't.

Chapter 7

The Final Act

The curse you can't escape

"You didn't start a band for the fame, the money, or the groupies. You started because nothing else sounded as cool... And you still haven't found a better excuse to skip real responsibilities."

- The Soundcheck Survivor

Too Late to Quit

At some point - probably around 2 a.m., standing in the rain, hauling gear into a rusted-out van that smells like beer and regret - you've asked yourself:
"Why am I still doing this?"
You've played to crowds that wouldn't fill a hatchback. You've loaded in through alleyways that should come with a tetanus warning. You've set up on stages held together by zip ties and hope, gotten "paid" in drink tickets, and watched the singer vanish to "chat with someone" the second it's time to load out. You've carried amps up staircases built by sadists, driven five hours to a gig that wasn't worth the petrol, and left venues with nothing but tinnitus and a half-eaten slice of pizza abandoned on your amp. And yet - somehow - you're still here. Logically, none of this makes sense. A regular job, stable income, and functioning joints wouldn't be so bad. But logic left the building a long time ago. Something keeps dragging you back.

Maybe it's the high of a perfect set - those rare moments when the whole band locks in and, for once, no one's faking it. It's the roar of a crowd - no matter how small - screaming your lyrics back like they were born with them. Or just a habit. You've been doing this so long, you wouldn't know how to stop if you tried. Perhaps that's enough to justify the long drives, broken gear, unpaid rehearsals - and the feeling that you're still chasing something just out of reach. Because deep down - even through the noise and fatigue - a part of you still believes in it.

The Myth of Letting Go

You've sacrificed sleep, stability, and every sensible career path imaginable. You've spent more on gear than you've ever saved for rent. And still, you're chasing it. Why? Because there's always one more. One more song. One more show. One more "maybe." The belief that next time, it'll all pay off. The logic is flawed. The odds, microscopic. Still, you're refreshing your band's page like a dying heartbeat, hoping it'll kick back in. You tell yourself it's about passion. Self-expression. Proving something to the world. But let's be honest - it's about not letting go. You've been at this too long to call it a phase. The music isn't just what you do - it's who you are. And walking away would feel like silencing something that still has more to say.

Some musicians quit. They grow out of it, pack away the gear, and move on. You didn't. You stayed. Maybe because you're still hoping for a miracle, or maybe because no miracle is ever coming, and that's never been the point.

You've mastered the humble shrug when people ask if you still play. You smile like it's just for fun like you're not secretly planning your next EP while pretending to enjoy brunch. Your friends ask about 'that band' like it's a childhood illness you should've recovered from by now. You still get emotional about your first gig - even though it was at a burger joint, and the loudest applause came from a kid with ketchup on his face.

You won't admit it, but there's a part of you that's proud. Not because it led to fortune or fame - but because you never gave it up. You kept showing up. Kept writing, rehearsing, creating. Even when it made no sense or felt like no one cared, maybe that's what matters most. Not how far you've come, but that you never walked away.

Not Done Yet

You tell yourself you could stop. That maybe it's time. Get a real job. Retire the gear. Let your spine heal. Trade the backstage scramble for a stable life. But even as you say it, you already know: you'd miss it. Not the stress. Not the van breakdowns or the passive-aggressive band group chats. Not the endless soundchecks or the venues with flickering lights and ceilings that leak when it rains. But the moments.

The rehearsal where everything clicks, and you all glance around like,

'Wait... did that actually sound good?'

That one show where the crowd is really with you. The drunk guy who slurs,

"You guys rock,"

and for some reason, it hits harder than any review you've ever gotten. The adrenaline rush when the lights hit. The silence right before the first note. The chaos mid-set when something breaks, and you fix it in real-time, pretending it was part of the plan. The feeling after a show. Sweat-soaked, ears buzzing, mind blank, heart completely wired.

And let's not forget the part no one ever talks about. The invisible work. Every band has the one: the unofficial "Manager" holding it all together. Not by vote. Not by title. Just the one who cared slightly more than the rest. It starts small. A text here. A reminder there. Suddenly, you're printing shirts, emailing venues, chasing deadlines, and asking - again - if the album art is actually done. Not because you wanted the job - just because someone had to. No one applied. No one noticed. It just... happened. You ask about the CD. They say:

"I've done my part."

As if playing your verse two years ago somehow mailed the

finished product to everyone waiting.

The unseen effort behind every show, release, or half-finished project quietly defaulted to the one who refused to let it fall apart. And when no one takes that role? Things drift. The songs get recorded, the mixes gather dust, and the best work you've ever done sits untouched because the final steps - those boring, unglamorous, necessary steps - never got handled. It's not burnout. It's inertia. Everyone's waiting on someone else to move first. But despite the chaos and delay, the same stubborn hope keeps showing up. That maybe this time, it'll all line up. That someone will follow through. That you'll press the thing. Book the thing. Finish the thing. And even if you don't, you still believe in it enough to try again.

You'd miss the dysfunction too. The bassist, forever ignored until the silence makes him suspicious. The guitarist, living out his rock god fantasy while stomping through yet another overextended solo. The drummer, playing with the intensity of a man escaping a burning building, only to be blamed for the singer missing his cue. The keyboardist - if there even is one - essential in theory, but still treated like a background texture by everyone but the sound guy, who's apparently fluent in modular gibberish. The singer, swaying between divine inspiration and total misfire - depending on the mix. The sound guy, standing at the back, deciding your fate with a single flick of a fader.

And you. Still showing up. Still fighting for the next moment. Still proving - maybe to no one but yourself - that it still matters. Because it does. You don't do it for the recognition. There is none. You don't do it for the money. What money? You do it because music is the one thing that still makes sense when everything else doesn't. Because the right chord progression can break your heart and fix it at the same time. Because every time you think you're done, a melody sneaks back into your brain and whispers, 'Not yet.'

This isn't a phase. It's not a hobby. It's not something you'll grow out of. It's a curse. A calling. A lifeline. It's yours. Because no matter how much this life punishes you, nothing else feels quite as real. And maybe the whole idea started as a joke. Maybe it was the roadie who said,
"We should start a band,"
while duct-taping a cable to the ceiling. Maybe he didn't even play anything. But the name was good. The riffs clicked. The chaos made sense. And somehow... it worked.

So, play on. Not because you have to. But because you wouldn't have it any other way.

Still here? You might want to flip one more page...

The "Almost Made It" Appendix

So You Want to Speak "Musician?"

For when you have no idea

(what the hell anyone is talking about)

Welcome to the chaotic glossary of Fading Rockstar Syndrome. This isn't a lesson. It's a survival guide. Whether you're a confused reader, a new bandmate, or someone who just nodded through an entire rehearsal pretending to understand signal flow, this is your cheat sheet. No theory. No lessons. Just some of the lingo, jokes, and absurd phrases musicians throw around like everyone was born knowing what "phantom power" means. Use it wisely. Or just fake confidence and say, "It's all about the tone..."
It works every time. Let's get started:

Air Grab
A dramatic reach into the void, as if summoning something profound. Usually unnecessary. Always performed.

Amp
The sacred box that makes guitars, basses, and keyboards loud. Also responsible for most band fights over volume.

Arpeggio
Playing the notes of a chord one at a time. Sounds fancy. Useless in flirting.

Arpeggio Sweep
A fast, show-off move where the guitarist pretends to play something beautiful but is really just sliding down the fretboard like a kid on a waterslide - with more wrist flicks.

Backline
The mysterious pile of shared gear already at the venue. Usually includes one ancient amp, a few dead cables, a cymbal stand that leans like it's seen some things, and a sticky mystery pedal no one will admit to owning.

Band Chemistry
That fragile balance of friendship, passive aggression, and repressed rage that somehow holds your band together. Like a group chat that just happens to play music.

Band Group Chat
A digital warzone where no one reads messages until it's too late and everyone's already mad.

Bass Face
The involuntary facial expression made while playing bass. Supposed to show you're "feeling it." Usually, it looks like sinus pressure.

Blow the PA
What happens when someone turns up without warning, and the sound system dies a loud, tragic death. Followed by silence and finger-pointing. Usually followed by the phrase: "Wasn't me."

Boutique Pedals
Tiny metal boxes handcrafted by tone shamans in the mountains... Allegedly "transparent," definitely overpriced, and guaranteed to ruin your bank account faster than your mix.

BPM (Beats Per Minute)
The speed of a song. Also, a number the guitarist completely ignores when he's "just feeling it."

Buffered vs. True Bypass
The kind of argument guitarists get into when they want to sound smart but really just don't want to admit their tone still sucks.

Buzzkill Frequency (500Hz)
That muddy middle range everyone pretends to hear. When

in doubt, ask the sound guy to "cut 500" and nod like you know what that means.

Can I Get "More Me?"
The most requested monitor adjustment in history. Translates roughly to: "Please ruin the mix for everyone else."

Can I get the kick
Soundcheck code for: "Get ready to hit your kick drum until the heat death of the universe."

Casio Keyboard
The tiny, plastic keyboard of childhood dreams. Perfect for learning. Less perfect for world domination. And no, it won't make you sound like a rockstar.

Center Mic Syndrome
The belief that standing in the middle of the stage automatically makes you the most important person in the band.

Cheat Sheet
Your only hope during rehearsals when your bandmates forget the bridge for the tenth time. Not officially part of the drum kit, but emotionally essential.

Crowd Participation Required
When the singer points the mic at the audience, hoping for a glorious sing-along. What they get is off-key mumbling and confused stares.

Cue Fill
A musical nudge from the drummer reminding the singer where the hell he is in the song.

DAW (Digital Audio Workstation)
The software used for recording and editing music.

Pronounced *"daw"* (/dɔː/) - like 'dog' but cooler.

Delay Feedback
That beautiful, spiraling echo that adds atmosphere to a song - or turns into an accidental wall of chaos if you forget to turn it off.

Delay Pedal
A device used to repeat what you just played - in case the crowd somehow missed it the first four times.

DI Box (Direct Input Box)
A small but mighty device that connects an instrument directly to a sound system. The bassist's best friend, even if he has no idea how it works. Exists solely to terrify guitarists.

DI Levels
Something the bassist will pretend to understand while trying to avoid helping you carry gear.

Dive Bomb
That horrifying, squealing sound that makes it seem like the guitar is screaming for help. Usually played mid-solo for "dramatic effect."

Double Kick Pedal
One pedal. Two beaters. Half the effort. Zero sex appeal.

Drop C
A tuning where the lowest string gets dropped for maximum heaviness. Also, somehow, an unintentionally hilarious pickup line. ("Hey girl... you into Drop C?") Yeah. Find a better conversation starter.

Drop D
A tuning that makes everything sound heavier and angrier. Great for writing one riff and pretending it's 12 different songs.

Drum Solo
A misunderstood cry for attention often mistaken for a seizure. Sometimes, it triggers mass bathroom breaks.

Drum Trigger
A device that replaces your drum sound with something cooler - right before your laptop gives up.

Duct Tape
The holy substance that holds together your gear, van, stage - and band relationships. Used for fixing cables and feelings.

Encore
The moment the crowd demands "one more song!" and the band pretends they weren't already planning to play one.

EQ (Equalizer)
A tool used to tweak the tone of an instrument. Musicians pretend to understand it. The sound guy actually does.

Feedback
The deafening shriek that happens when a microphone and a speaker decide to have an unholy conversation with each other.

Filter Cutoff
The knob keyboardists keep adjusting during rehearsal, hoping someone will finally notice. They won't.

Fingerstyle
A way of playing bass that uses your fingers instead of a pick. Can be smooth and subtle - or a phrase you definitely shouldn't say at a bar.

Fix It in the Mix
The studio version of "I'll deal with it later." Used to excuse sloppy playing.

Floor Tom
The low, thunderous drum that sound guys somehow always mute by accident. Or on purpose.

Frankenstein Kit
A drum setup built from mismatched, questionable parts. Part gear. Part chaos. Entirely functional - mostly.

Fretboard
The part of the guitar you stare at while pretending you're not completely lost in the middle of a solo.

Front of House (FOH)
The sound system for the audience. Also, the sound guy's control tower - where he manages your mix and quietly questions your entire existence.

Frontman Energy
Equal parts adrenaline, delusion, and hair products. Can also manifest as an urgent need for multiple scarves.

Germanium vs. Silicon
Two types of transistor materials that guitarists claim sound different, even though no one can actually tell unless you're tone-testing in a vacuum with headphones made of ego.

Ghost Cave Reverb
That moment when the singer's monitor mix turns their voice into a swirling vortex of regret.

Ghost Note
A subtle, almost-inaudible drum hit that nobody in the audience will ever notice... but drummers will die defending.

Gig
A live performance. Could be at a massive festival or a dingy basement with a broken PA system and three audience members (mostly friends of someone from the band).

Gig Hangover
The combination of exhaustion, emotional damage, and tinnitus that follows every show. Cure: unknown.

Glory Note
That one high note the singer might hit live if the stars align, the humidity is perfect, and the sound guy doesn't hate them.

Goes to Eleven
A reference to Spinal Tap, the greatest rock mockumentary ever. It means turning something up beyond its actual limits.

Groove
The rhythmic feel that makes the music move. Bassists live for it. No one else appreciates it.

Guitar Face
A facial expression suggesting deep emotion, but usually looks like indigestion mixed with spiritual awakening.

Guitar Spin
When a guitarist swings their instrument around their body. Looks amazing when it works; hospital visits when it doesn't.

Guitar Creep
When a guitarist increases volume mid-set, in tiny increments, until they've colonized the entire mix.

Half-Stack
A 100-watt amplifier setup designed to make sure no one else on stage - or in the venue - can hear anything but the guitar.

Harmonic Squeal
That squeaky high-pitched noise guitarists hit mid-solo to prove they've mastered the art of unnecessary flair. Also, when they want to sound impressive - whether it fits the song or not.

Hair Flip Timing
A precise form of stage choreography where the singer flips their hair to the beat, often at the emotional climax of a song. When mistimed, results in regret and whiplash.

Hi-Hat Clutch
A small but crucial piece of hardware that only fails during important gigs. Like clockwork.

High-Pass Filter
A magical knob the sound guy uses to clean up your tone while pretending to care what your amp sounds like.

Hospitality Rider
The sacred scroll of unrealistic demands bands make before a show. You asked for water, snacks, and three kinds of hummus. You got a broken chair and a coupon for chips.

Input List
The sacred scroll of what gets plugged in where. If you lose it, prepare for chaos and at least one mic picking up alien transmissions.

It Sounded Better at Practice
The universal excuse for a bad performance.

Kick Drum
Also known as the bass drum. Provides the heartbeat of the song and all of your lower back problems.

Laminated Chart
What you bring to rehearsal when you're tired of being blamed for everyone else's memory problems.

Latency
The delay between pressing a key and hearing the sound. Causes existential dread, missed cues, and trust issues.

Line Check
The mini panic rehearsal right before the set - where everyone makes random noises, pretends to know what they're doing and discovers half the gear doesn't work. Not to be confused with actual preparation.

Load-Out Vanish
A sudden disappearance technique perfected by singers during gear load-out. Often blamed on "talking to someone."

Making It Big
The mythical dream of becoming famous through music. Usually replaced with becoming regionally known to 48 people and one podcast host.

Metronome
A click that keeps time. Universally hated by guitarists and singers. Worshipped by drummers. Feared by chaos.

MIDI (Musical Instrument Digital Interface)
The special, slightly unstable language of electronic music. Used by keyboardists, producers, and tech wizards to control sounds - until it randomly stops working five minutes before the show.

Midrange (Mids)
The frequencies your guitarist swears are "missing" - while overpowering everyone else.

Mic Check (Singer Edition)
Not a technical test. A full mini-concert involving vocal runs, emotional gestures, and a dramatic whisper no one asked for.

Mic Drop
When a singer drops their microphone for dramatic effect, often met with instant regret from the sound guy.

Mic Stand Lean
A calculated posture that screams, "I'm emotionally available and also maybe better than you."

Modular Synth
An expensive spaghetti monster of wires, knobs, and blinking lights. Capable of incredible sounds and complete emotional breakdowns.

Monitor Mix
The on-stage sound that lets musicians hear themselves. The primary source of endless complaints.

One More Song!
The phrase every frontman dreams of and every other bandmate dreads.

Overdub
When a musician records extra parts over an existing track to hide their mistakes.

Passive-Aggressive Tension
The default communication style in most bands. Especially visible during rehearsals and group chats.

Patch (Synth Patch)
A saved sound setting on a keyboard. Every keyboardist has 700 of them and uses three.

Patch Cable
Tiny cords that power your entire tone... and betray you the moment you try to look cool.

Pedalboard
A collection of guitar effects pedals that take up half the stage. Causes 70% of onstage tripping hazards. Guitarists will mortgage their homes for more of them.

Pedalboard Jungle
The tangle of wires, stompboxes, and shattered dreams guitarists build to avoid practicing actual dynamics.

Perfect Tone
The imaginary sound guitarists are chasing when they buy their ninth overdrive pedal and say, "Just one more."
It does not exist. But they will never stop looking.

Phantom Power
The mysterious electricity that powers certain microphones. Despite its name, it has nothing to do with ghosts or the supernatural - no matter what unholy sounds the singer is making.

Phase (It's Not a)
The thing you've been doing for twenty years that your relatives still think you'll grow out of.

Pinch Harmonic
See: *Harmonic Squeal*. Also known as "the note that accidentally makes a dog bark."

Placebo Fader
A fake adjustment the sound guy pretends to make so musicians stop talking.

Post-Set Delusion
The moment after a great show when you consider quitting your job, selling everything, and touring full time... Don't.

Power Ballad
The emotionally charged, slow-building anthem designed to make the audience feel things - usually regret.

Power Fill
A massive drum run designed to impress the audience - or cover up the fact that the guitarist forgot the chorus.

Power Stance
The classic wide-legged stance that screams, "I mean business."

Premature Exit
When the singer leaves the stage triumphantly before realizing the song isn't over - results in standing awkwardly near the drummer until the outro ends.

Rehearsal
That thing the band was supposed to do before the gig. Often replaced by vague texting and last-minute panic.

Reverb
The effect that makes vocals sound like they were recorded in a cathedral, cave, or public restroom. Singers always want more of it.

Reverb Revenge
What the sound guy dishes out after too many unreasonable requests: drowning the singer's voice in echo until it sounds like a haunted cathedral.

Reverb Tail
The lingering sound after a note ends - heavenly when right. Horrific when it swallows the band.

Ride Cymbal
The subtle, shimmering cousin of the crash - perfect for finesse, until the sound guy deletes it.

Scale
A sequence of notes used to build melodies, solos, and lifelong guilt in musicians who never learned them. Comes in many flavors: major, minor, exotic, and "whatever I just played by accident." Still the fastest way to fake your way through a jazz conversation.

Session Player
Shows up, nails it, disappears. The audience assumes he’s just there to fix the Wi-Fi.

Setlist
The sacred document outlining what a band thinks they’ll play. Printed, laminated, and ignored by song three. Bonus points if the singer holds it up like ancient scripture and asks, “Did we play this one yet?”

Show Up, Tune In, Zone Out
The bassist’s unofficial motto.

Signal Chain
The audio path from guitar to amp, often overcomplicated to hide the fact that the guitarist has no idea how EQ works.

Signature Move
A frontman’s go-to theatrical gesture - includes the Slow Turn™, the Point™, or the classic Crumpled Emotional Collapse™. Often rehearsed. Never admitted.

Slap
A percussive bass technique involving thumb smacks and finger pops. Sounds amazing in funk. Sounds like someone dropped a wet steak onstage when used in rock. Bonus cringe if it happens during a serious breakdown.

Snare Check
The one soundcheck moment guaranteed to rupture eardrums. Usually occurs exactly when someone is mid-sentence.

Snare Drum
The sharp, cracking drum that makes everything feel punchy. Also, the only part of your kit anyone ever compliments - if you’re lucky.

Solo (Bass)
Rare. Often unplanned. Sometimes accidental. Occasionally glorious.

Solo (Outro Edition)
An extended farewell to musical structure. The song ended two minutes ago. The solo did not.

Solo (Unsolicited)
A sudden, often extended moment of guitar self-indulgence. Happens during rehearsals, soundchecks, or any quiet moment that wasn't about them.

Solo Until Sunrise
A fictional band where the guitarist never stops soloing. No one else in the band has been heard since.

Soundcheck
The pre-show ritual where bands pretend to adjust things and act like they know what they're doing. The sound guy pretends to listen - and quietly tries to make them not sound awful.

Stage Dive
When a musician or an audience member hurls themselves into the crowd, praying they don't get dropped.

Stage Fashion Logic
If your outfit lets you breathe, walk, or sing comfortably - it's not rockstar enough. In other words, if your outfit lets you breathe, you are doing it wrong.

Stage Plot
A diagram showing where each band member stands onstage. Ignored immediately when the singer starts wandering.

Stage Presence
What the bassist doesn't have until something goes terribly wrong.

Stage Real Estate War
The silent battle between the singer and everyone else over who owns the front of the stage. Fought in mic stands, monitor positioning and pure willpower.

Stage Throne
The drummer's seat. Sounds regal. The least comfortable stool you'll ever spend hours on.

Stick Bag
Your sacred pouch of wooden salvation. If lost, you might as well be a singer.

Synth Pad
A soft, sustained sound that adds emotional depth and cinematic flair. Tragically ignored by everyone except the guy playing it.

Tech Support (Band Edition)
Read half a manual once. Now blamed for everything that doesn't work - including the drummer.

Technical Difficulties
A magical phrase that explains everything from gear failure to forgetting the lyrics. Covers all sins.

Tetanus Venue
Any gig location where touching a doorknob feels like a health risk, and the stage may collapse mid-set.

The Last Fader Drop
The moment the sound guy quietly reminds you who really had control all night.

The Mix
An imaginary concept where all instruments are balanced, and everyone is happy. Has never actually existed outside of a studio.

The Pact
A silent truce between the sound guy and whichever band member asks for the least.

The Soundcheck Survivors
A tragic band who never made it past soundcheck. Still tuning. Still arguing about the monitor mix.

The Void
What happens when your entire synth rig crashes mid-set. Also describes the internal panic you try to mask with a calm nod.

Tom Roll
A rapid-fire drumming moment that either saves the song… or triggers an unintentional solo.

Tonal Vision
When a guitarist refuses to turn down because their 'tone' depends on the amp being loud enough to crack drywall.

Tone
The holy grail of guitarist obsession. No two players agree on what it means, and that's precisely how they like it.

Tone Chasing
The never-ending quest to find the perfect sound. Involves buying expensive gear, hating it, selling it, then rebuying it full price six months later because "it actually sounded kinda good."

Tone Sculptor
What guitarists call themselves to justify 17 fuzz pedals and a

sound no one even noticed.

Too Much Reverb?
A philosophical question posed by singers moments before they drown in it completely.

Tuner Pedal
Silently mutes your signal so you can tune between songs. Ignored completely - until someone throws shade or a bottle.

Tuning (Drop C, Drop D, etc.)
The passive-aggressive way guitarists argue about musical identity while secretly hoping someone notices their string gauge.

Turn Down
The thing no guitarist has ever done voluntarily.

Turn Me Up
The guitarist's eternal plea. Usually ignored.

Turn the Drums Down
The sacred chant of audio engineers and anyone within a 3-block radius of a rehearsal space.

Unsolicited Tech Talk
What musicians think impresses the sound guy. It doesn't.

Van Smell
From hell. A unique blend of sweat, spilled coffee, fried food, fear, and broken dreams. No matter how many air fresheners you use, it never truly leaves.

Vintage Analog Synth
A keyboard older than your uncle. Capable of one good sound and 73 terrifying ones. Loved anyway.

Vintage Tubes
Old, expensive glass components guitarists believe hold the

soul of tone. Most people just hear amp buzz. Guitarists hear destiny.

Vocal Fry
That croaky, gravelly tone singers use to sound "emotional." Sometimes it's art. Sometimes it's just a cold.

Vocal Warm-Up (Real Version)
Scales, breath control, hydration, discipline.

Vocal Warm-Up (Singer Version)
Random yelling, sipping whiskey, whisper-singing to the mirror - and blaming the mic when the high note collapses in protest because reality didn't match the drama.

Wait, do you control the lights too?
The single most offensive thing you can say to a keys guy.

Wah Pedal
A foot-controlled effect that makes a guitar sound like it's trying to speak dolphin. Often used to drown out your best drum moments.

We Had a Record Deal Once
That one band who casually drops "we were almost signed" into every conversation. And has been doing so for 15 years.

Whoa, that looks complicated.
Polite audience-speak for: "I have no idea what you're doing back there, but it involves a lot of blinking... and probably controlling the traffic lights too."

XLR Cable
The big, round-ended cable that microphones use. If a singer doesn't know the name, they're not allowed to complain when one breaks.

Xtreme Volume Syndrome

The uncontrollable urge to keep turning up until someone walks out or goes deaf. Often affects guitarists.

You Rock, Dude!

The one compliment the singer will replay in their head for the next six months - no matter how sarcastically it was delivered.

That's it... You now speak almost fluent "musician."
If you understood every joke, you've been in this game too long. If you didn't, don't worry - neither has the singer...

Now flip back to the beginning.
Reread.
Recoil.
Relate.
Because this life never really ends.

You just keep tuning up...

Table of Regret... and Occasional Glory

(because apparently... structure matters)

Chapter 1: The Master of Blending into Oblivion

Playing bass in a band full of attention seekers

Chapter 2: The Human Metronome

Loud, sweaty, and one broken stick away from a meltdown

Chapter 3: The Shredder in the Spotlight

Six strings, one giant ego, and an amp that goes to eleven

Chapter 4: The Alchemist of Airwaves

A sonic architect lost in his own world

Chapter 5: Center of the Universe

A Legend in His Own Mind

STILL NOT
FAMOUS
BOOKS

www.ingramcontent.com/pod-product-compliance
Lightning Source LLC
LaVergne TN
LVHW091145080826
845145LV00008B/2260

* 9 7 8 1 7 6 4 0 6 4 8 0 4 *